ASEMIC
WRITINGS 2

ASEMIC
WRITINGS 2

La Mancha -The Unforgiven

MARK URIZAR
ZBIGNIEW JAWORSKI

To order additional copies of this book, contact:
Xlibris
AU TFN: 1 800 844 927 (Toll Free inside Australia)
AU Local: (02) 8310 8187 (+61 2 8310 8187 from outside Australia)
www.Xlibris.com.au
Orders@Xlibris.com.au
823704

CONTENTS

Where does this great evil come from?

Foreword

Our present is inextricably linked with our past and future.

In this second volume of asemic tales, the story of a tortured soul - La Mancha is recounted through many single-page compositions with fluid drawings and scripted words. This is a seemingly-familiar tale, an age-old story, long suppressed within the human consciousness, finally surfacing to reveal a tainted past with an awful accompanying truth. It is foretold that this tale will continue to linger in our thoughts until all that has been ordained occurs.

Each page and asemic composition opens a small portal to this tale. Each provides some interpretation of the suppressed truth. Each reveals how our past is continuing to influence and determines who we are and become, and what occurs and will occur, ultimately revealing all there ever was, is, and will continue to be.

La Mancha's life is a set of many past bad choices, decisions, and actions that enabled evil to manifest here on earth. What La Mancha had done cannot be undone, disguised, obscured with fiction, or diluted by time.

This is a tale of a stained soul sentenced to live a miserable and cursed existence, forced to reconcile all the bad that was done. As this tale is told, it also reveals our truth, who we are, have become, how we have contributed to what is occurring, and how we all will also be destined to search for redemption, salvation, and forgiveness.

The Permanent Stain

Throughout time, there was and always will be the stain.

The stain is a shapeless entity that has always resided here. This is an ancient evil that manifested into life at the dawn of time. It is also part of the duality of our existence, a direct opposite to goodness, and keeps all that exists in balance.

The stain appears when the alternating cycle of life turns from good to evil. Then without notice, it emerges, creeping from the darkness, latching on to and corrupting all innocence and goodness with its negative energy. Like a contagion, it then spreads rapidly, consuming all it can before the alternating cycle again changes, which then forces it back into waiting.

History has never acknowledged the stain's existence. There is no verified record of what this evil had done or the destruction or death it had caused. Survivors of the stain's wrath were all bystanders, far removed from the evil it unleashed. What they saw, they did not understand or believed possible; rather, they thought this was fate, providence, and God's will enacted on earth. The stain is part of all the evil that exists. It is also a part of our life. We nourish it as we succumb to sin. All our misdeeds, transgressions and all the bad we do enables it to grow and become powerful. It then comes as a powerful unyielding force that radiates its negative energy, overwhelming all with misery, misfortune, and death. This dutiful servant of death also comes to sway and tilt the cosmic balance, so earth is darkened, and life plunges into conflict and war. This it does until goodness again returns, overpowering evil by redeeming and reconciling what it had done.

We all know the stain exists. We know this because, for eternity, it has accompanied us. And deep down, we all dread its imminent return, fearing the devastation it has promised to unleash on us. I know this evil. I have seen and felt it as I am stained and damned. I have carried this within me for eternity and cannot dispel it. I also know its redeemer – karma, which is now holding me to account, punishing me for being stained and a servant of evil.

La Mancha – The Place

La Mancha is a place located in Central Spain. Named so centuries ago, meaning 'the stain', indicating the place where evil had once resided.

La Mancha, the name, first appeared on maps in the tenth century, during the Northern African Moors' invasion of Spain. The initial pain of conquest felt by the Spanish was merely a precursor to the carnage that would follow and envelope Spain in war. Then for centuries, the Moors and Spanish fought many bitter battles to control and retain Southern and Central Spain.

Spain's innocence was slaughtered and killed as the war escalated. Many heinous acts followed, releasing substantial negative energy. This awoke evil and enabled the stain to manifest. It then came quickly, grew, and strengthened, becoming a large formidable evil force. It then began to expand, rapidly progressing, enveloping the countryside, decimating homes, villages, communities, and then cities. This, however, did not stop the fighting or killing.

War was feeding and growing the resident evil, the stain. Soon people realised evil was residing in La Mancha. It had settled there. All that once thrived died, and everything good, was corrupted. The stain's presence and its rampant evil had cursed these lands and caused an imbalance that tilted the order of things. This imbalance then forced its redeemer, karma, to intervene, thus beginning an epic battle between good and evil that lasted centuries. The fortunate, those who survived, were the people who had fled the cursed lands. These survivors then also named the place La Mancha to warn others of the stain's presence and curse.

At the end of this tale, there were no winners, and there was no recourse. Everyone at La Mancha had suffered. Goodness suffered by unleashed evil and evil by the retribution karma had sought. The continuous fighting had also decimated the Moorish empire and Spanish nation. What occurred was not recorded as all who survived wanted to forget this dark chapter in history. Soon all that remained was the name - La Mancha, which in time also lost its meaning. Centuries later La Mancha would again gain some notoriety when Miguel de Cervantes published his 1605 book titled *Don Quixote de La Mancha*.

La Mancha Reborn

This may be history repeating itself, but for me, it is my reality, my life.

Things had been too good for too long. Life was easy, and complacency had set in. Sin was rife, and people no longer lived a just or meaningful life. People had become selfish, uncaring, and what they did was self-serving, which often flouted the eternal universal laws. This then caused a cosmic imbalance, triggering a series of events causing history to repeat itself.

Many ominous signs had appeared. All indicated something was nigh. No one, however, believed. All the ancient knowledge was lost, forgotten, or disregarded. All had optimistically thought nothing bad could happen and resigned themselves to accepting God's will.

There was no awareness or preparedness for what was to occur. An ethereal seismic shockwave preceded this, my birth. This disrupted and ruptured the social balance to enable evil to manifest with me. This traumatised and affected my community. People soon knew something was not right. My parents sensed this at my birth and ominously chose to name me La Mancha. This name, I have since carried all my life. It defines me. I am my parents' stain.

From birth, my presence caused stress, misery, and misfortune to all who came near me. People soon realised this was not arbitrary but fated. Many then knew I was stained, by name and by evil within me.

Years would pass before the evil I had within me could be contained; this only occurred when its redeeming force, karma, manifested to sentence me for my past sins.

I am that cursed soul, a stained individual who has evil within. For this, I am the unforgiven, now destined to live a sentenced miserable life. I am being punished for allowing evil to stain my soul and for sins from a past I don't recall. Evil and my stained past had followed me here.

My Stain, My Karma, My Sentence

I was born deformed and destined to live an institutionalised life. When I had sufficiently matured and realised this, envy overtook me and became me. I was envious of others.

Unable to walk, I wished I too had a healthy and strong body. As I wished this, the wonders of modern science and medicine began working on me. I underwent many painful medical procedures and operations. Doctors eventually reshaped and cured my body. This was what I needed and what I had wished for. When this all ended, I could finally walk.

This miracle, however, did not change my fate or the sentence karma had in store for me. Cured, I felt blessed. I also found I had second sight. This gift gave me clarity in thought and an ability to regress and relive previous lives and times. I could often wonder in thought by considering the many different possibilities while also exploring how the universe worked. Soon, however, I found this was no gift but also a curse.

My thoughts and mind then changed. I began focusing solely on the bad I had done. Soon the horror of my past consumed me. My waking hours became unbearable with horrid thoughts always occupying my mind, continuously and constantly replaying the evil I had unleashed on others.

I soon understood who I had been and what I had done. I had been a mischievous, hardened, corrupt, and stained soul that purposefully had unleashed evil onto others. I had caused great suffering, calamity, destruction, and death, extinguishing all the life I could. And despite this being in the distant past and long-forgotten, karma had not forgotten nor forgiven. Rather, karma sought out to punish me as a perpetrator, sentencing me to life. The only blessing was that karma's presence had quelled the evil within me. It, however, still lives, thrives, remains strong, and has the power to overwhelm and devastate when it chooses. This, I must stop. I need to dispel this evil so I can also cleanse my stained soul.

The Karmic Force

All the bad I had done now weighs heavily on my mind and soul.

The untold pain and suffering I had caused is now deeply imprinted on my mind. Karma has resurrected the memories of all my past misdeeds, which now replay to torment me, each brings some evil that seeks to corrupt my mind and body. As it lingers, I often see this appear on my body, surfacing on my skin as festering sores that I then carry as scarred flesh. This past is now trying to define who I am.

Karma had come to collect a debt that was past due.

Karma is that powerful unyielding force that holds wrongdoers to account. Rather than helping or supporting those in need, it manifests to set things right and restore balance. When it sentenced me, it also freed me from the cursed evil had placed on me. I now know karma. I feel its presence and know it will remain with me until my end. I also feel the evil within. I feel its malevolent force radiating and discharging from me. I see people close to me suffer, affected by its presence. This evil is strong, powerful, and still able to corrupt innocent souls. Mostly it seeks sensitive and receptive souls, those it can temp with desires to sin. This is how evil survives and thrives.

People who succumb are controlled and manipulated so they harm others, and then devastate their own lives. Evil only leaves when it is finished, leaving shattered people beyond redemption, fated to die a painful death. This reality, I have long known and endured. I am unable to stop this or help those in need. This has become part of my reality, my life, my karmic sentence.

I sense it will take many lifetimes to complete this sentence. I know it will never be commuted, nor will I be absolved. I must, therefore, reconcile and atone all I can while I can. I don't want to fail as this would relegate me to purgatory for eternity.

The Life Sentence

My name means bad luck. My presence disturbs people.

In the distant past, our ancestors had ancient knowledge that foretold when evil would reincarnate or manifest in their midst, within their clan and community. With this knowledge, they could sense the forbiddance and coming of evil. They had learned to recognise and read cosmic signs that foretold its coming. They could interpret birthmarks on parents and baby, together with ominous planetary alignments, to determine when and where a stained soul would be born. They would then ensure the stained soul was either cast out or confined to a solitary life in prayer, forced to repent until they dispelled the evil they had. These stained souls were purposefully separated from society to contain the evil and not allow it to grow or strengthen, thereby not affecting the innocent.

By the Middle Ages, the religious doctrine had replaced this ancient knowledge. For a time, stained souls were still forced to live solitary lives in prayer. They were placed in isolated temples, monasteries, and convents. Confined in prayer, people mistook these stained individuals as holy. Not knowing or understanding the truth, people revered their commitment and sacrifice. These stained souls then became priests and ministers. Rather than bringing salvation or benefits to the masses, they cursed their followers for having trusted them. And as this misguided reverence continued, evil strengthened and began to affect society. The loss of ancient knowledge had blinded us. We no longer could recognise or see the forbidding signs of the coming of evil. Rather, we were taught that evil does not exist. We were also taught misery and misfortune are part of the divine plan, God's will, and chance occurrences are part of life. Mathematical probability reinforces this, making everything possible, probable, and not set, or given. I, however, know different. I know the truth.

I am stained because I had caused untold misery. Many people suffered and died because of me. And I still affect many with the evil that radiates from me. I have seen how this evil tempts and how people succumb as they falter and corrupt themselves. Their lives then spiral into the abyss, taking everyone close with them. I see this happening to everyone I have known. This is my curse.

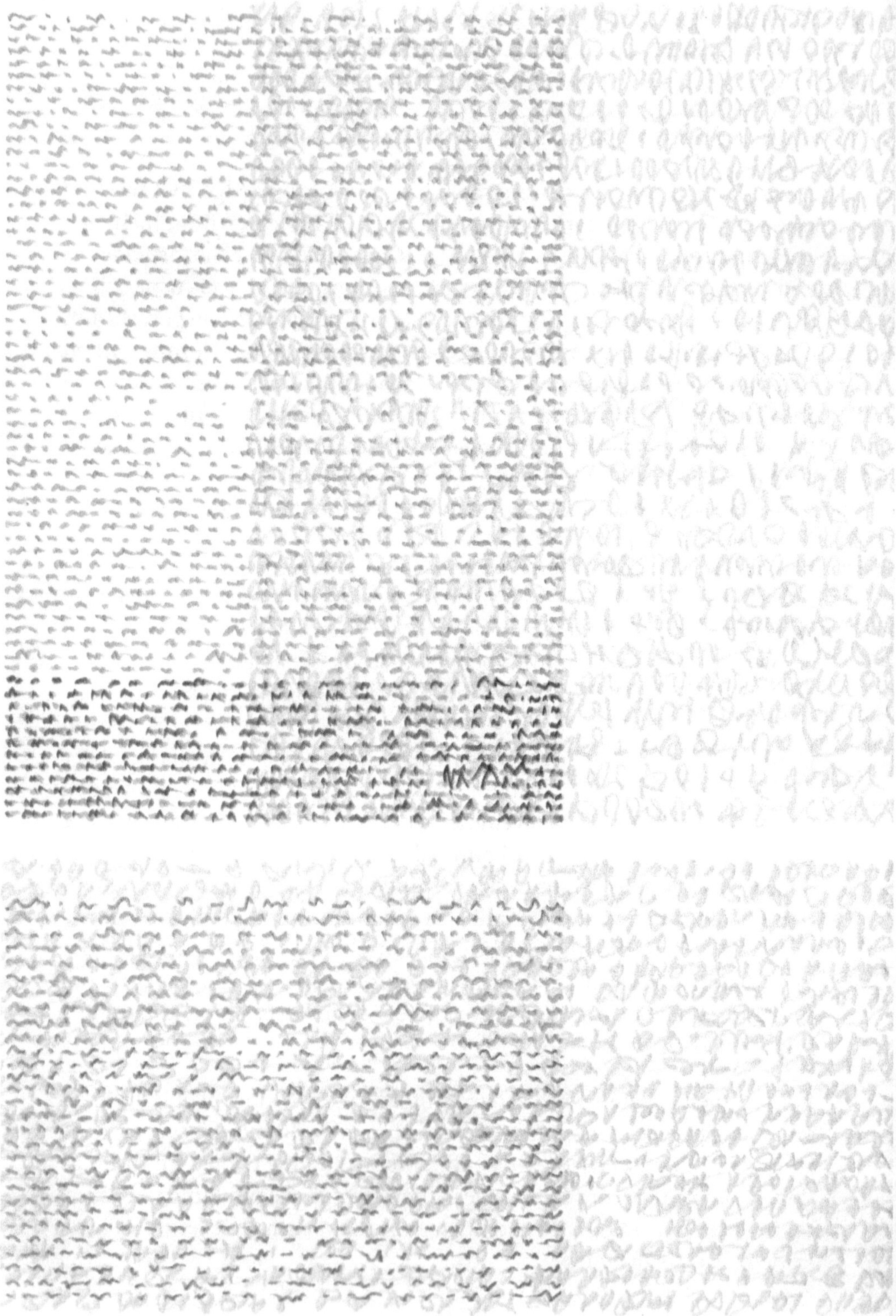

Remembering the Beginning

That was then, this is now. I am the new generation, born to a new era, at the start of a new dawn.

Before I arrived, my family was carefree and happy. And when I finally arrived, I was not the blessing they wished for but their curse. I did not want to be reincarnated here, to these people, at this time. But karma had forced this. It had placed me here to harm this family. My mother knew. She later told me I was a mistake, caused by a cosmic misalignment that enabled evil to manifest.

Stained, I brought misery and misfortune into this world.

I came stained. I came with evil already within. As soon I arrived, it began radiating its malevolent, corrupting force from me. I saw many people suffer, including my parents, siblings, and many others close to me. Soon people avoided me. They also regretted my birth. I became their stain too. I had brought bad luck to my community. I had shackled everyone close to a miserable existence.

At age three, my mother ran away. She left me with my father and two elder brothers. Life then became unbearable, without purpose or progression. My father soon disowned us, his children, unable to cope. The misery I carried then extended far and wide, as I was relegated to aunts, uncles, cousins, and anyone who would take me. Eventually, there was no one willing to care for me. Disowned, I was placed in foster care, thinking this would free me, but soon realised I was abandoned, left homeless, and destitute. I quickly learned to disengage and disassociate from the reality of daily life. This enabled me to endure and survive the ordeal of living a stained life. I found within an alternate reality, an altered state of being, where I could venture at will and ease my pain.

With the second sight afforded to me, I ventured deep into my past. I relived many past incarnations to see what was. There, I found that my two brothers had accompanied me for eternity. They had always been by my side, with me at each incarnation, despite me always harming them. And they always forgave me, faithfully following me to wherever I went. This, I have never appreciated nor understood until now. I must seek their forgiveness to reconcile this.

Born to Repent

Deeds are eternal, unlike mortal life.

I had accumulated substantial karmic debt that had come due. I had let this accumulate by failing to reconcile my past. This had forced karma to intervene, to hold me to account. This is why I am now punished and sentenced to life. This is my fate and destiny. There will be no pardon nor any possibility to commute this sentence. Nor will I be able to escape this life sentence as I must endure this to its very end. And while I do, I have been given the chance to redeem myself and reconcile all the bad I had done.

What had I done?

My second sight enabled me to understand who I was and what I had done. There, I saw and relived my past with all my misdeeds. I relived this by allowing each memory to overtake my senses and engulf me with some past trauma. This was not easy but hard, nor was this a blessing. It was my curse. As I peered deep into the past, all I saw and relived were the horror of who I was and what I had done. I am a product of a brutal unforgiving past. I was forced to fight to survive in each life. I always struggled, suffering from life, feeling relentless trauma. This had hardened my soul. The only relief I found was within the darkness of my soul, my shadow side, within the most primordial, regressive, underdeveloped, and unenlightened elements within me. These strengthen me and gave me an avenging resolve. This was when evil also found me, entered me, took control, and did what it wanted. Since that time, I have carried the same evil within. I know it intimately.

My second sight has shown me who I was and what I had done. I was always attracted to negative energy as moths are to light. With the evil within, I was always tempted and succumbed to vices and sin. I was and still am selfish, lustful, greedy, envious, angry, and my mind is always filled with hate and rage. I have uncontrollable pride and envy that is beyond reproach. This is who I am, immoral and corrupt. And this is why karma intervened, to stop me and contain the evil I have within. Karma had ensured this by caging the evil I have within so it can no longer control me. All I feel now is an ongoing struggle within, as the evil tries to break free and again, control me.

Adolescence

I was naïve, delusional, and arrogant. I felt entitled, thought I was invincible and knew everything, yet felt lost. This became my childhood and youth. I did not understand life or logic. By adolescence, I felt a powerful force within begin to dominate and control me. It then overtook me, and transformed me into a narcissistic adolescent brutish savage. I became hateful, loathsome, and a true incarnation of some evil rancour.

Thinking back, I felt like someone else was living my life. This was a self-centred evil entity whose mind was consumed with vengeance, anger, darkness, and self-pity. As I endured this, it became me.

As I matured and gained a sense of self, I no longer could accept who I had become. I had to control the raw emotions and primal anger that occupied my every thought. I also had to contain the explosive energy that often burst, spewing raw anger out. I needed help. I needed to be saved.

I could not contain or quell what I had inside and neither could others help me. Dismayed, I let sloth become me. I trapped myself in a self-loathing state. There, as I saw how flawed I was, I lost interest in life and no longer cared to be saved. I became transfixed with inaction and would not change or progress. I had become the essence of laziness, idleness, and indolence. I had dishonoured life, my body, my being and humanity by becoming some pathetic inert sluggish matter that consumed life.

Karma then intervened. It had waited for me to sufficiently mature so I would understand the sentence it gave me. Karma had quelled the evil I had within and forced me to change. This was when it took hold of my life and began punishing me incessantly until I changed my condition and mind. Once freed from this, my sluggish hindrance, it then sentenced me. As it did this, I was not resentful, angry, or spiteful. I needed karma to intervene. I needed to change. Karma then placed me on a learning journey that I alone must make. It allowed me to rehabilitate myself by repenting and atoning for all the bad I had done. To do this, I needed to learn to apply judgement, wisdom, understanding and use all the knowledge I had so I would succeed. At the end, if I reach redemption, then I may be able to dispel the evil I have within, along with all its anger, hatred, and deep-seated contempt for life. This will be my payback for what this evil had done to me.

Dreaming

During my youth, when I slept, my dreams set me free. I could be where and who I wanted to be. Nothing held me back, I was without inhibition, I was carefree, and I did as I wanted. I accessed, ventured, explored, and experienced all the different realities my dreams offered. There, I found relief from this miserable mortal existence. Soon all I wanted was to continue dreaming forevermore. This had removed me from life with its despairing thoughts. There, I could bypass all the miserable hardships that life presented me. As I sought to dream, I started hibernating to sleep forevermore.

Karma intervened again. Karma did not want me to waste away, nor did it want me to be comforted. It had come to ensure I was reminded of the bad I had done. Soon I dreaded dreaming.

My dreams had become torturous and nightmarish. Each started with incomprehensible ancient tongues chanting, slowly intensifying, and regressing me to some distant dark past. I then started reliving all the bad I had done. I found myself doing horrid acts, causing harm and death. At each dream's end, the consequences of the evil I had unleashed unfolded before me, revealing the devastation I had caused.

One dream regressed me to my childhood. I had arrived at my mother's funeral. There, I felt a cold wind blow, chilling me to my core. I began yelling, 'Don't leave!' only for darkness to befall and envelope me. I was then taken to a different time, seeing people shuffling through my meagre possessions, finding lost letters that I had written to my mother but not sent. Then I heard someone say my death was just punishment for causing my mother's death. A piercing white light then temporarily blinded me, only to find myself in a temple of sorts. Before I entered, an overwhelming stench momentarily held me back. There, I saw hundreds, thousands of decaying, mutilated, dismembered human body parts. I sensed I had orchestrated this sacrificial ritual. I found myself laughing uncontrollably as I led victims to death. I heard each plea change into a deafening scream, as each victim suffered a more horrid death than the last. Somehow then I had I thought this was justified.

Now each night this dream always replays. I now recognise all the anguished faces and remember each deafening scream.

The Eternal Yearn to Sin

From darkness, we are born, and so we try to return to it. Like moths to light, we are all attracted to darkness.

Everything crumbled, and I faltered when life kicked me hard in the gut. I had succumbed to temptation and reverted to the dark side. I had followed evil underground. I found myself in the familiar, was attracted to evil, and joined many other stained souls. We dealt with drugs, extortion, prostitution, and murder. This was what I knew and remembered. This felt like home. I felt whole again. Here, I could magnify my evil and help unleash its intent on earth. As I sinned with evil, karma soon intervened again. It came and retaliated, proceeding to severely punish me for my audacity and disobedience. After a while, I awoke. I realised I had been comatose, left in a coma. Excruciating pain then overwhelmed me as I felt a large sutured sore on the side of my body. Surgery had been performed to remove and transplant one kidney. I then knew there would be no shortcut, no clemency, nor reprieved from this miserable existence. Nor could I expect a quick end. Karma would now control me to my end. Dismayed, I then understood this could happen again if I again faltered. This was the futility of defiance.

Death comes only when it chooses.

These misdeeds had reset my fate. What I had done now had become perpetual. My past had now again intertwined itself with my present and reset my future, beginning a new punishment regime. As day turned into night, the day's punishment ceased, then nightmares began to haunt me. And as night then turned into day, and the haunting nightmares ended, new mental and physical punishment began. This became my fate, my life. I simply had to persevere with this. This was my doing. I had marooned myself here at this critical juncture, at a precipice in time, stymieing all further progression and transforming my sentence into an anguished mental journey. This, I must now endure. My salvation lies not with my death but with me reconciling what I had done. I cannot again try to prematurely change my life or stray off the path or lose hope. This will only damn me further, possibly for eternity. I must, therefore, remain focused, steadfast, use all my means, might, and inner strength to pay my karmic debt.

The Evil at La Mancha

Why is the region in Central Spain called La Mancha?

In AD 711, Muslim Arabs from Northern Africa crossed into Europe, invading the Iberian Peninsula. During the next seven years, they conquered Portugal and Southern Spain. Somewhere in the middle of Spain was La Mancha. This had become a battlefield, a killing ground, where Spanish resistance was quashed and slaughtered. The local population tried in vain to protect their kin and property but to no avail. The invading Arabs, known as the Moors, ensured no one survived. Whole communities were taken prisoner, tortured, and then slain. Those not immediately beheaded or burnt were said to be taken back to Africa as slaves, only to be drowned en route in the graveyard depths of the Mediterranean Sea.

The purposeful slaying and massacring of people without mercy continued for centuries. This killing had awoken evil, which began to seed. It manifested as the stain, which quickly grew and became a powerful intimidating force. It then settled at La Mancha, as it proceeded to establish its will on earth, corrupting and staining all it could.

After 380 years, the alternating cycle between good and evil had finally turned, this was when evil's redeemer, karma, manifested into existence. Karma had come to La Mancha. It had come to restore balance by cleansing and removing the resident evil from these lands. This then began a saga and epic battles between the Arabs and Christians and good and evil. This was also when the Moors' power began to wane. It would, however, take a further 400 years for the Moorish empire to end, but this did not end the war between good and evil.

Spain's suffering would continue for another 300 years as the church applied its inquisition powers on those who had survived the Moors. It did this by progressively and systematically cleansing the lands, reclaiming lost souls, removing all traces of the Muslim faith, and returning these stained lands to the Christian faith. This ended in 1826 when the inquisition executed its last damned soul.

Remembering Past Misdeeds

If all my past misdeeds appeared on my skin, I would be an ugly mess.

As I find myself living and suffering a karmic fate, I sense many others are similarly fated. I remembered one, Don Quixote de La Mancha.

Has this become my reality, my fate, and my life? Am I like Don Quixote? Have I allowed the insanity of my reality and dilemma to consume me? Have I forced this punishment on myself? Why must I reconcile and atone for a past I don't recall?

As I wake, fragments of my past fill my mind and begin occupying my thoughts. Karma makes me remember so I don't forget. Unlike Don Quixote, I cannot fantasise out of this fate or existence. Nor can I choose a different life or live an alternate or imagined reality. Nor can I forget or clear what replays in my mind.

The memories I have are ancient. These extend back generations, recalling countless past lives. In each, I see myself focused on evil, destroying and causing death. I was vengeful, cruel, and had a righteous immoral nature. I had focused on maximising chaos, trauma, and harm to life. I made people vulnerable and then my victims. I had weaponised my pride, arrogance, and egotistic self to needlessly corrupt the innocents I had enticed. I had an evil persuasion that affected, impacted, and damned many people, even the most powerful.

My second sight showed me how voraciously and relentlessly I had pursued and caused death. I started unprovoked conflicts and participated in wars only to quench my unholy desires. I harmed all I could, combatants, civilians, the guilty and innocent alike. I did not discriminate. I had a vengeful, lustful, unfulfilled heart, yearning to feel and taste human blood. I felt how darkness within had consumed and changed me. I had become a formidable malicious force that yielded to none. I had become a messenger of death.

I now know evil had completely corrupted and stained me. I was damned beyond redemption. By me seeing and reliving this, I now understand why karma had to intervene and stop me. As it holds me to account, I feel I am changing as I travel along this path towards redemption. I must confront and reconcile my horrid past so one day I can be forgiven.

Spain Consumed

The Moors' invasion and rule of Spain began when Tariq bin Ziyad crossed the Strait of Gibraltar to decisively defeat the Visigoth King Roger at the Battle of Guadalete. This was in AD 711. The defeated Spanish were then subjugated to Muslim oppressive rule. Many struggled to assimilate, most resisted, fought, and the majority perished.

Europe and the church had turned their backs on Spain and its people. Some 300 years passed before Europe mobilised against the Muslim faith. This, however, occurred a continent away, with the Crusades venturing into the Middle East, wanting to reclaim Jerusalem. And as this injustice led to another, this began a perpetual and endless stream of conflicts and wars that consumed people and resources for centuries.

After 800 years, the Moors' rule ended. At the end, there was no victor nor benefiter. Everyone who participated lost and suffered. The Moors returned to Northern Africa and settled in Mauritania and Malias and became known as the Arab-Amazigh ethnic group.

Spain fared no better. Its lands were filled with traumas and victims. Europe also suffered, strained by unending wars in the Middle East.

By AD 1291, the city of Acre fell, which then ended the era of the Crusades and ousted the church from Jerusalem. To recover, the church then chastised the Crusaders, charging the Knights Templar in AD 1307 with heresy. They were then tortured, many killed, and the crown confiscated their wealth and possessions.

The inquisition then consumed Spain, subjugating all its citizens. All beliefs were challenged and questioned while not knowing what was truly right or wrong. The only guidance afforded was indecipherable with Latin text forced on an illiterate population.

Centuries passed before the rampant killing stopped and peace again prevailed. Time then cleansed these lands; all the bad was eventually atoned, reconciled, and forgiven. The stain had vanished, along with all thoughts of vengeance, wrath, anger, and retribution. These had long been replaced with empathy, compassion, and love. Time had also changed and transformed the Spanish nation into its present pluralist society with the blended cultures now thriving at La Mancha.

My Relapse

How can I reconcile my past?

What I had done has already occurred. I cannot change this, nor will I be reprieved or forgiven for this. All I can do is persevere with what lies ahead of me.

I know what I must do, but I hesitate and procrastinate. I delay and falter as I am weary and exhausted. My journey has been long, hard, and arduous. To persist, I am forced to remain vigilant and not sleep. As I peer into the distance, I see a forbidding and treacherous path before me. I am however tempted to veer off course as I succumb to my tiredness. My body needs rest and comfort. And as I rest, I find myself regressed to a time I had previously succumbed to this temptation.

Is this a test? Am I to redo my journey?

My mind is weak, unable to focus. Fear soon grips me as I think of the consequences of relapsing. This heightens my anxiety and begins to overwhelm me, soon jolting me back to my harsh reality. There, I remind myself, despite this life journey being without end and, possibly, will take an eternity to complete, I must however persevere and reach redemption. As I continue, my weariness stymies my progression and kills my motivation. This is my failing. This is how I succumb to my idleness with a desire to rest. This, I must overcome and change to progress. I need to focus so as not to inadvertently prolong my journey or damn myself further. I must continue and complete this journey by myself. I cannot rely on others or ask for help. Nor can I be absolved from what I had done. I must trust myself, find my inner strength, and be determined so I can persevere to my end.

This thought cleared my mind. I find I am no longer tempted to sin. Freed, I allow providence to take me where it will. This lesson of patience and abstinence has brought me here. I now know I will not relapse again or give cause to karma to intervene and punish me further. Nor will I divert from this path or choose a different life. I have finally found what I had sought. I found freedom within my mind, allowing me to ponder in thought. With this, I contemplate what could have been if things were different.

Shadow Revealed

Peace and calm will prevail when evil yields and is driven deep underground. Evil, however, cannot be defeated or erased. Like goodness, it is an eternal force that will always exist. When it leaves, it hides and hibernates, waiting to be resurrected. As it waits, it continues with its business and rituals so it can again flourish. It tempts all with false hope so it can seed, grow, strengthen, and overwhelm.

Those who worship it wait patiently and eagerly for its return. They wait to be commanded while dutifully rehearsing and enacting satanic rituals to fuel discontent and hatred in society. They entice and coerce the gullible and innocents to join and participate, so as to fill ranks with corrupted souls. This evil spares none, not the newly born, old, or dying. And nor does it stop or give reprieve or any leniency to the suffering. All that this evil will touch will wither, suffer, and die.

Evil had once enticed me. My participation had corrupted and stained my soul. I was initiated and became its pathological servant, encouraging all to expand evil on earth. I wished with this evil that innocence would breathe its last breath. I was complicit with evil intent. Evil had immersed me with sin, giving me the desire to kill and end life. This became my focus, my aim, and my life.

This occurred when evil emerged from the darkness, no longer able to control or contain itself. It came with an unquenchable thirst that drove it insane with a vengeful desire for revenge. Hungry for blood, it overwhelmed lands and people with a furor that sickened and corrupted goodness. This was AD 720, the start of the Reconquista wars at La Mancha.

I found myself there with evil already within me. It had already taken my mind and life and was controlling me. Even today I feel its presence. It is alive, strong within me, still able to overwhelm me and envelope me with its darkness. Even with its redeemer, karma, close by, this evil is still formidable, being an eternal powerful force that can only be contained and caged and not erased.

The Struggle

Why are there such repressive forces in this world?

Everywhere I look, I see repressed people. A ubiquitous force exists here that does this: preventing and stymieing progression and peace. This force has ensured every step taken forward, must be fought and won. This, we all must do so not to become victims of this force.

I have seen what occurs when people quit. They quickly falter in despair that overwhelms and then damns them. Many don't recover or return.

Persistence is, therefore, key to progress and surviving this life. Each day must be hard-fought, a struggle, and a challenge to remain on the path that leads us to our destiny and end.

I have always struggled with patience and persistence. Without hope or purpose, I have no motivation, and so I procrastinate. I let time slip by without toil until again I am forced to act as new challenges confront me. Then desperation grips to overwhelm me again, testing my resolve to continue.

Why do I feel so repressed? Why is my mind filled with so much dread?

This is my life, each day filled with endless, eternal challenges, each becoming an ordeal that I must confront and overcome. I delay while knowing I have no choice but to continue, so I endure and try to stay on course. This occurs as evil within me tries to hold me back, while karma forces me to move and progress. Both are here, waiting to see how this journey will end for me.

I cannot vocalise or tell anyone of the tension I have in this life and what I must endure. No one would believe that I have caged evil within that stymies my progress while radiating its malevolent intent. Nor would anyone believe karma has sentenced me. Most think life follows God's plan and will, dismissing bad luck as chance occurrences by some quirk of fate. I know different. I have seen and felt both. I know both exist as I struggle with each, each tests my resolve and stymies my progress.

The Futility of Resistance

Karma had ensured there would be no reprieve or relief for me. I am destined to feel each moment of every punishment. This, I must learn to endure until the end of my sentenced life.

I am sentenced for having unleashed evil on this world. What I did had disrupted the divine plan. It tilted the balance against good, allowing evil to resonate throughout the centuries. What I had done eternally stained me, each life lived, each incarnation. My bad also forced karma to intervene, to break this cycle and stop evil from repeating itself.

Evil had placed me out of sync with life. It separated me from my kin, my people, and all I previously knew. It placed me on a divergent path and trajectory, one that led me to damnation. Evil had given me everything I wanted: power, wealth, and status. I also had country, religion, culture, and law on my side. With this power and authority, I began to unleash uncontrollable anger and rage on everyone around me. I did as I liked, and all I did was selfish and self-serving.

This was when my envious pride drove me with destructive urges. Evil had become me. I ritually corrupted and damned everyone and everything I knew. I also became the messenger of death, willingly sacrificing my family, siblings, heirs, and friends, all to appease my ego. I wantonly endangered life to feel and taste the fear that preceded death. This was when I forced everything living to decay into death. Soon all that once was good and thrived withered and died. And when people retaliated and challenged or accused me, I diverted blame to the innocent, who then suffered needlessly. I was beyond reproach and redemption, no one could help me.

This was my past. My many misdeeds had, however, outlived my flesh. Who I was and what I did damned me. All I have now are the reoccurring nightmares of misdeeds that replay constantly in my mind. With these, darkness still envelopes me, and I often succumb to temptation and desire. This is when my ego, my shadow, arises from within to further corrupt and stain my soul. Now sentenced, I have to transcend this by finding new purpose and hope.

The Crusades

By AD 1095, as the Moors continued with their conquest of Spain, Pope Urban II persuaded the faithful at the Council of Clermont in Southern France to free Jerusalem. This foreign land was their Promised Land.

The pope proclaimed saving Jerusalem was a right and moral cause. People then rallied, took arms, and so began the Crusades. This then quickly escalated from conflict into war, taking all Europe's armies to the Middle East.

From AD 1096 to AD 1291, eight major Crusades ventured into Jerusalem. Fighting ensued with untold terror as death was unleashed on the region and people. The Crusades were not fighting to protect Christendom but to dominate and control Jerusalem. The Crusaders quickly learned and transformed themselves from volunteers into highly-trained killing machines.

The Crusades unleashed unbridled wrath on all who lived in Jerusalem— all in God's name.

In AD 1120, this quest received royal legitimacy when King Baldwin II and the Patriarch Warmund sent nine Christian knights to protect pilgrims travelling to Jerusalem. With a blessed royal decree, this group rapidly expanded, attracting many to their cause. Soon this group became an elite fighting force, with military status. They distinguished themselves by not retreating or surrendering in battle. They were known as the Knights Templar, the fiercest and most heroic warriors of Christendom.

By AD 1300, the Jerusalem cause had faltered. After 300 years of war, nothing was gained. All had lost substantially, including the church and monarchy. To recover, the king manipulated France's legal system to annex lands and expel or imprison anyone who could harm the crown. The king first targeted the Jewish population, confiscating their wealth and expelling them. Then by AD 1307, the king targeted the Templars. He coerced the church to charge the Templars with heresy and then proceeded to arrest, imprison, and kill them while confiscating their wealth.

Desensitised

The evil I have within has progressively and substantially worsened my predicament. This is an emanating evil force that often intensifies to discharge substantial negative energy that overwhelms all within its reach. This, I cannot control or stop. Nor can I confront or challenge this evil inside as it quickly retaliates by magnifying its power to cause me immeasurable pain that disables me. Nor can I tell anyone or seek help. I simply have to endure to survive this ordeal.

How can I explain what I have inside? Would I be harmed, killed, or banished by society? How could I account for or reconcile the trauma others felt and experienced?

I have seen and felt the pain and suffering that emanates from me. I know everyone in my community has felt and experienced this. It comes as an intense, powerful, and vengeful force. This, I feel within, as its palpable anger grows, escalating with desperation as it tries to also consume me. This evil knows the instability of its situation and fears that one day it will be dispelled, forced to dissipate back to the ether, to its origin.

Numerous times I saw and felt this evil climax. I saw and felt it unleash its full might with raw, unbridled power to harm and extinguish life. I saw this force decimate people, destroy families, and cause mass social upheaval. I saw this evil also disrupt social order by causing substantial turmoil and crisis within businesses and government. Then there was no immediate remedy for what had occurred and no mercy shown for those who suffered. No righteous being, just behaviour or goodness, could have changed what occurred. Nor could anyone prevent or stop this evil.

The Evil Within

Where does this great evil come from?

At every opportunity, evil tries to gain a foothold on this physical plane. It has tried for eternity to manifest into reality. It uses everything it can to influence and devastate. Misconstrued simple benevolent acts and innocent questions seeking answers to what is right, good, or moral often open portals into evil, allowing falsehoods to be promulgated and believed. This enables evil to seed, germinate, grow, and eventually dominate the unsuspecting yet receptive hosts. With this foothold, evil then begins to manipulate life and consume goodness. It will use all its means to tempt, entice, and then sway life by promising salvation but delivering damnation. The power evil has is great.

Littered through human history are many occurrences where goodness withered to give rise to great evil. Such events are also often intertwined and mixed with seemingly-moral and religious acts, so as to blur the distinction between what is moral, right, and yet also evil. The Crusades were such an agathokakological act. These enticed the innocent and the faithful into a religious undertaking that led to conflict, war, and then death. The church's backing and blessing had concealed its real purpose. Only centuries later were the true horrors and unspeakable evil acts known. What occurred only ensured differences between good and evil can never be fully reconciled or resolved, creating a struggle that continues without resolution or end. This is also my eternal struggle. I cannot easily distinguish between what is right and wrong. When I return to the light after succumbing to temptation, it is always temporary as I thereafter lose myself to the depths of darkness within.

The evil I carry is still strong and relentless, never stopping, seeking always to gain some foothold in life. And as karma stymies its plans, I feel its palpable anger grow. And as I try to dispel this evil from me I do so by thought, wishing to dismember it slowly, part by part. But what I think then happens to me. These thoughts dismember me from within, making me bleed and suffer. This, I must accept, endure, and overcome before I can dispel this evil I have within.

The Spanish Inquisition

The Spanish Inquisition was infamous for its persecution of innocent people. It targeted Christians, Jews, and Muslims alike, seeking to find heretics. This, it did by torturing innocent individuals until all confessed so they could also be justifiably executed. The inquisition began in AD 1184 when Pope Lucius III sent bishops to Southern France to track down the Catharists, a group of non-Catholic Christian heretics. The church proclaimed it was acting on God's will, trying to stop evil on earth. This began a process that consumed people while the church benefited from the property it confiscated, which it then used it to gain influence and favour with the powerful. The church amassed substantial wealth that allowed it to expand its reach, power, and authority. It started granting favours and doing the monarchy's bidding, including persecuting minority groups and removing opposition. With this, the church had diverted from the righteous path and lost its way.

By AD 1307, Philip IV, the king of France, persuaded the church to charge the Templars with heresy. Inquisitors then mass-arrested and tortured some 15,000 Knights Templar. Many were executed. Despite being the fiercest, wealthiest, most powerful, and revered military order of medieval Europe, the Knights Templar were no match for the unbridled greed, lust, and revenge the king and church had unleashed on them. The church then did the unconscionable: In AD 1431, it allowed the inquisition to burn at the stake its most famous victim, Joan of Arc. This revealed the depth the church had sunk, sparing no one with its pride and envy as it used its authority to unleash an unstoppable vengeful force that eventually executed some 32,000 souls. The initial aim of the church may have been to restore order, unify lands, and purify Catholicism, but this was long forgotten. The sin of greed had changed the church's intent. The power and wealth accumulated by the church revealed its disregard for human life and its sinful nature. This left no doubt the church had misused its divine authority and lost its moral compass. Left unchallenged, the church had corrupted itself by doing what it liked, applying inconsistent, arbitrary, and contradictory processes that were far removed from the sacred scriptures. With this, it gained an evil arrogance that the church retains to this day.

Dissociation

This home is no longer mine. I am no longer welcome there.

The sun shone and warmed my back as I step through the threshold. This used to be my home. I had always gravitated back here. This was where I had spent my youth. All my childhood memories were here. It was my haven. I felt safe here. And yet now, as I enter this place and pass through the threshold, overwhelming anxiety takes my mind and fills me with dread. As I ventured further, my senses dulled and darkness enveloped me.

I remain calm and wait until I regain composure and am fully cognizant. Soon my anxiety and apprehension vanished. I feel strangely cleansed. I try to think but find I no longer remember who I am or where I am. I feel lost and confused. People then start to congregate around me, overwhelming my senses, and panic grips me again. I struggle to remain calm. I feel a tear of sweat roll down my brow. Then I notice one person approach me, place their hand on my shoulder, and say, 'It will be all right'. I smile and look around, acknowledging those who are now glaring at me. I, however, don't recognise anyone. Anxiously, I look for a quick exit but find myself seeking refuge within the anonymity of the growing crowd. This, again, overwhelms me, so I cannot speak or interact. I let myself become the crowd but think this is not where I want to be. Then I feel an unexpected warmth and calm envelop me as I again see sunshine stream in from a partly-blinded window.

This jolts and awakens me. I try to comprehend what just happened and remember this dissociation is something that regularly happens to me. It is part of my condition, something I cannot change, avoid, or correct. This is a sort of temporary amnesic memory lapse that I regularly experience and have long accepted as part of my reality. This is just one of the many challenges I need to endure. Resisting or treatment does not help and would only prolong my dilemma, and cause me more suffering. The only hope for me is to wait for the sun to again shine on me, dissipate this reoccurring fog that often clouds my mind and release me from this condition.

Forgotten Emergence

My life journey began two generations ago. I had manifested when my mother was conceived as a mere cell in my mother's ovaries and remained there until birth. During the intervening years, I had felt and lived each of my mother's hopes, dreams, dramas, and experiences. I truly thought I was my mother. I felt all she felt and knew all she knew. I felt and lived her essence. This I remember clearly.

I had genetically inherited everything from her. This has since defined me and enabled me to live this burdened mortal existence. But I am not her. I am unlike my mother. I lead a different life and live in a different era. And despite not having the freedoms she had, I feel contented with what I have and with what she has given me. It was my mother who gave me the means to endure this arduous, challenging life and the ability to steadily learn, gain new skills, and change as I progressed.

While I remember and know this, I have no childhood memories of my mother from after birth. All were corrupted as if she did not exist. I don't even remember her face, and nor do I remember all that happened when she was with me during my youth. All that I remember is before birth, along with every previous incarnation I had lived and every misdeed I had done.

How is this possible? Why were the memories of my mother corrupted? Why can I only remember the deep past but not my youth?

I had always wanted to remember how I had emerged into this life and what I did during my youth. Often I try by concentrating and focusing on my youth but to no avail. All I seem to recall are corrupted pieces, memory fragments of some past I don't remember. This is, however, all I have. This is how my life has unfolded and defined me.

The loss of my early childhood memories has greatly affected me. I know this is common. There are many similarly-fated people who also persevere without knowing their immediate past and seem to know everything else. But for me, without knowing my immediate past, I feel I am unable to know who I truly am.

Past and Future Envisioned

I know my presence and appearance cause distress to many. What people see, however, is not me but the evil that exists within me. They possibly see an angry, resentful, and vengeful person who uses all available might and means to cause chaos and mischief. Try as I might, I cannot change this perception. Nor can I dispel the unwelcomed evil entity that resides within me. I do sense the evil I carry within is progressively diminishing and losing control, but it will not leave. It persists by continuing to reach out, damning other unfortunate souls. This is how evil continues to project its misery onto this world.

I keep moving, travelling while I can. This ensures the evil I have and carry does not affect those near me. Misfortune, however, never leaves me. It follows me and at times envelopes me to again ruin all I had achieved. Only when I am completely isolated and there are no people around me this evil loses interest and hibernates. Solitude then enables me to contemplate, gaze into the past and future, looking for clues so I can understand this life. My second sight however does not allow me to see my immediate past. Rather, it takes me to the distant past and future. The past is fixed, but the future remains in a state of flux, which constantly changes and evolves. I have seen many plausible futures unfold. In one, I have seen society's end. To this end, we all had participated and contributed to corrupting society entirely until it collapsed into extinction. We had all succumbed to greed and unsustainable processes that then short-circuited life here on earth. On the other end, the most appealing plausible future revealed an evolved society based on goodwill, participation, consensus, and well-being. This society had dispelled its evil and was filled with benevolent and just people who had become everything they ever wished to become. What I had gathered from these visions is that we still have time. We can all choose the future we want and we can do this by fighting for what is right. We can use our social might to place humanity on a just and sustainable path. But as I stop thinking and contemplating, all I see is inaction. I cannot influence or change what will occur. All I can do is continue to live my sentence life and pay my karmic debt so one day I will be freed and forgiven.

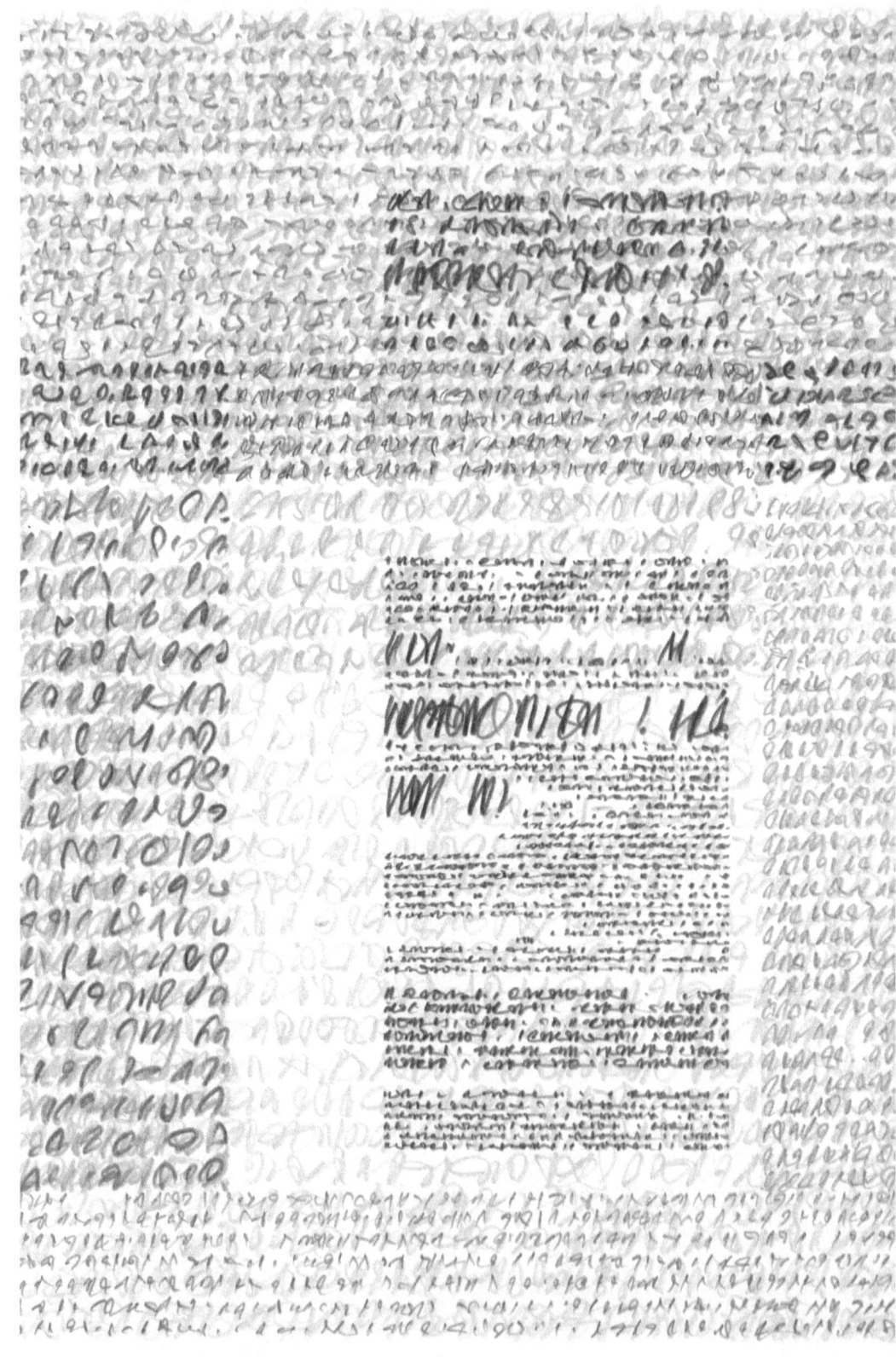

The Enduring Stain
on the Landscape

La Mancha may be famous for the story of Don Quixote, but few knew of its ominous past.

The Islamic faith began to spread when the Master of all Messengers, the Prophet Muhammad produced the Quran in Mecca. Soon the Muslim faith enveloped the Middle East and later parts of Europe. By AD 720, the Moors had already expanded the Islam faith deep into Spain and Southern Europe. The Moors' war machine had enabled this, as it also progressively removed all opposition.

As the killing and fighting ensued, an evil awoke, which began feeding on the negative energy released from all the death, misery, misfortune, destruction, and all the badness, and horrid things people were doing to one another. This manifested evil was the stain.

As the stain strengthened, it spread and moved as it also consumed goodness and corrupted the remaining innocence with desires to sin. It then began to also stain people, society, the countryside, and the lands, corrupting and eventually extinguishing all remaining goodness. The lands then dried, the water disappeared, and the landscape became arid and inhospitable. What was once bountiful and beautiful became barren, desolate, and forbidding.

This is what occurred at La Mancha, which had disrupted the divine plan. Evil had manifested and caused a cosmic imbalance, which then forced providence to intervene, sending karma, its redeemer, to restore order. Battles between right and wrong, good and bad, karma and evil then continued for centuries, each seeking to dominate the other. The malevolent forces were formidable as they had already grasped, stained, and damned every living thing.

The evil that manifested at La Mancha had also gripped the Moorish empire. The Moors succumbed to sins of pride and vengeful envy. Caliphates became delusional with power. As each sought to expand their rule and dominance, internal infighting ensued, which quickly escalated into private battles fought to settle worthless scores. Then 800 years after the initial conquest, Moorish unity and empire fractured and collapsed, ending their rule and domination of Spain.

The End of the Empire

Centuries of fighting at La Mancha had stained the lands. Evil had gained form, manifested, and secured a firm foothold on this plane. Evil then proceeded to consume innocence and replace goodness with misery, sin, and death. And as this happened, the order of things tilted, causing an imbalance, forcing karma to intervene and retaliate. This was when the epic battle between good and evil began. The alternating cycle of fortune and misfortune had just turned and began affecting all life on those lands, including the powerful Moorish empire.

The Moorish rule ended in AD 1492. There was no unified Christian uprising, rebellion, or heroic act that defined this moment or ended the Moors' conquest. Rather, karma intervened to dispel evil by cleansing and removing the stain from these lands. The corrupted and unrepentant souls who participated suffered; all were sentenced to live miserable lives while forced to atone for their sins. The less fortunate were already damned, consumed by hatred; they were well beyond redemption. These damned souls now face eternity in hell.

Today the lands at La Mancha are no longer stained. There is no rampant evil causing mischief, chaos, conflict, or misfortune. Nor is there suffering at La Mancha. The karmic debt incurred by the people who lived on these lands has been fully paid, allowing peace again to prevail.

History has wiped clean the centuries of fighting that marred and scarred the landscape at La Mancha. No one remembers the epic struggle and there are no reminders. All the relics from that era are long lost or forgotten. This long-forgotten, forsaken distant past has since been replaced with peace, goodness, and prosperity.

54

The Human Emergence

While Steven Dawkins gazed up at the stars to understand the universe, we looked deep within, into our souls and hearts, and saw who we were.

The most archaic humans, our ancestors, emerged from deep within the earth when this world moved from the Mesozoic into the Cenozoic era. Life had just evolved from its reptilian past into mammalian domination. While many species perished, our ancestors persisted, surviving near extinction, as they chose to live on the surface, between the heavens and earth. At first, they sought stability, salvation, and meaning, trying to understand life. As they searched, they also spread, scattering and settling across all six sacred directions. In time, they learned to adjust to circumstances and began to harvest the goodness from the landscape. Then as they accumulated property and wealth, they also began hatching plans to change and control the world.

This is our past. It has been defined by our nature and who we are. Rather than finding balances on earth and protecting other species, we demoted the entire nonhuman world to a soulless assembly of atoms and resources to be used and consumed. Any protection we afford is only for our benefit. This, our disregard for nature and the nonhuman life, continues to this day. It has since become abundantly evident with resulting climate change that we are, indeed, pushing life to the brink of extinction.

As centuries passed, we progressively and purposefully transformed everything natural into commodities, consumable products, waste, and more people. This is our selfish, self-serving nature that also carries the belief that we have a God-given right to dominate and consume. Greed is our vice of choice, using this as an instrument to exploit nature while causing worldwide extinctions.

We have placed ourselves on a path of self-destruction. It will soon be too late to repair the damage we have caused. We all know how this can be corrected. We all have heard the message, and yet we all fail to heed this or act. This has become our choice. We will wait until redemption day, which will likely come after the damage occurs. This will seal humanity's fate. Karma will then intervene, as it has done in my life. It will come to ensure we all then suffer as we pay.

An Angry and Jealous God

I have wronged You, God, by worshipping others. I repent and reject these false gods so You can accept my penance and forgive my sin.

The greatest sin of all is to worship a false or rival god. There is only one true God that deserves to be worshipped. He alone created us, and He alone placed us here on earth, generation after generation. So He alone has the right to be worshipped.

There is only one God. He is not your or my god—He is the God.

We separate ourselves from the divine when we sin. By deliberately disobeying God's will, we also deny Him. God, with His infinite wisdom, has allowed this. He has given us free will and the choice to decide our fate. And despite seeing and knowing our true nature and the desires that exist in our hearts, He does not intervene, and nor does He stop the bad we do. This, He allows along with all the suffering from all our choices, conflicts, and wars, so we learn. Evil thrives with the freedom we have. It forever tempts us with desire. It is always present, always testing our resolve, always tempting us with the desire to cause mischief. It is then our choice. We alone allow evil to enter our souls, corrupt us, and stain us. We all know this is wrong. We all know we must then repent and atone for our sins to redeem ourselves. And if we fail to do so, then we also know someday we will be held to account and feel God's wrath.

O Lord, I have so sinned and wronged You. Forgive me and bestow Your mercy upon me! I have so forsaken You by worshipping false idols and vices. Please forgive my sinful nature.

We reveal our true selfish and self-centered nature when we ask Him to accept our failings and wrongs and forgive our sins. This is our pride that has eroded our faith. It allows us to question Him and then think that He does not listen or care. And as we lose hope, we also begin to separate ourselves from God. And this, He does not condone. The path to redemption is long and arduous. Forgiveness is only reserved for the obedient, truthful, and those who repent the wrong they do. These are the people who live just and righteous lives. This is what I must do. I must reconcile the bad I had done, repent and atone for my sins before I can redeem myself, and ask for His forgiveness.

The Stained Jerusalem

It took 700 years to reconcile the evil the Moors had unleashed on Spain. A world away, in Jerusalem, a different tale was unfolding.

Jerusalem is an enigma. It is located at the nexus between extremes of goodness and evil. These two extremes are equally powerful, kept in balance by each other, as none can dominate. This dichotomy, the Jerusalem story, is also a reflection of the human journey. We are blessed and stained; we struggle with all the good and bad that exists.

Jerusalem was first settled in 4500 BC. By 1000 BC, the Kingdom of Judah became Jerusalem which transformed the region into a major trading center. Soon the Egyptians, Philistines, Arabs, and Ethiopians envied Jerusalem. Thus began centuries of fighting driven by vengeful greed that sought to secure, control, and then profit from Jerusalem.

The centuries of sieges and battles that followed were with the Assyrian (712 BC), Babylonian (586 BC), Alexander the Great (332 BC), Maccabees (164 BC), Roman Republic (63 BC), Byzantine (AD 614, 629), Crusaders (AD 1099, 1187, 1192, 1244), the Mongol Empire (AD 1260), Ottomans (AD 1624, 1840, 1887), World War 1 (AD 1917), Arab-Israeli War (AD 1948), and the Six-Day War (AD 1967).

None of these conflicts and wars resolved differences or settle disputes. Rather, the centuries of fighting seeded resentment and distrust between people, religions, and nations, ensuring there would never be compromise or peace. This remains a true reflection of us, our human nature, revealing just how conflicted our lives are as we all struggle with a life that oscillates continuously between good and evil.

The Blessed Jerusalem

Jerusalem is a sacred and blessed place. History has recorded many miraculous holy events there. Each had cleansed these lands. Each also inspired and seeded spiritual thinking that then established the three most dominant faiths.

The blessings received at Jerusalem established the Kingdom of Judah, which enabled the Judaism faith to thrive. In 957 BC, the first temple, also known as Solomon's Temple, was constructed in Jerusalem. This had replaced the original tabernacle constructed at Sinai by Moses. And as the cycle of life kept oscillating between good and evil, this temple was destroyed and rebuilt several times. In 586 BC, the Neo-Babylonian Empire destroyed the first temple, which then was rebuilt 71 years later and destroyed 445 years later by the Romans in 70 BC.

And before the second temple could be replaced by a prophesied third, Christianity challenged the Judaism faith by seeding itself in Jerusalem. In 6 BC, John the Baptist was born, and later Jesus was presented at the temple mount. It then took another 400 years to construct the first Christian temple: the Eleona Basilica on the Mount of Olives. The construction of many other temples soon followed, including the First Church of the Holy Sepulcher on Calvary (circa AD 335), the first monastery on the Mount of Olives (circa AD 380), and the Church of the Holy Zion (circa AD 394).

By AD 610, Islam began dominating Jerusalem with salat prayers held on the temple mount, soon to be followed by the construction of the Al-Aqsa Mosque (circa AD 625), the Dome of the Rock (circa AD 687), and the Masjid al-Aqsa (circa AD 705). Other denominations then followed, also building their temples, the New Church of the Holy Sepulcher (circa AD 1149), the Lutheran Church of the Redeemer (circa AD 1898), and St. George's Cathedral (circa AD 1899).

All the temples constructed in Jerusalem have encapsulated in stone the human faith. They also reflect the human condition and our religious journey. They have captured who we were, what we thought, and what we believed in.

The Sinful

Our sinfulness and brokenness have separated us from God.

A sinful nature has firmly entrenched itself in our souls and hearts. The freedom we have and the choices we are given can corrupt and damn us. It is solely for us to choose what we do. Often it is not our choice, as our self-serving and selfish nature drives and dominates us. This is when we succumb to our deepest desires. We all know this is wrong, and yet we fail to do what is right.

We will all wrestle with temptation at some time. This is when we must choose to be moral, righteous, and steadfast and not succumb to desire. This is when we must remain true and on a path that enables us to fulfill our destiny. However, if we persistently make wrong choices, then the fluid duality that exists will take us to its evil extreme, only to abruptly leave us with the consequences of our bad choices. At this end, karma will likely also intervene to ensure we reconcile and settle our accrued debt of evildoing.

Despite all our good intentions, as individuals and as a society, we will, nevertheless, always succumb to temptation and desires. Our sinful, egocentric, self-serving nature has always influenced us with its narcissistic thoughts that often develop an evil intent. Unable to reason with this, our selfishness and solipsism corrupt us further, taking us to places we would not otherwise go and doing things we would not otherwise do. This departure from goodness then frees us from the thought of consequences. Repercussions no longer matter, nor do thoughts of the harm we may unleash on others. And by not being held to account and by not redeeming ourselves, we may later dismiss and forget this evil we had done, but karma will not.

All the bad we do is remembered as accrued karmic debt. This cannot be erased, negotiated, or cancelled, even with death. This is a debt that remains with us until it is reconciled and paid. This debt also has a set limit; when reached, it must be settled. Karma will then intervene to hold our sinful nature to account. It will sentence us to a life full of suffering, misery, and misfortune. This we will need to endure until all our past sins and misdeeds are atoned, reconciled, and we redeem ourselves.

The Complacency Vice

The capitalist-governed world has become complacent. There is no need to struggle or rebel against oppressive rule. We have become wealthy, contented, and have attained many privileges, living free, selfish, self-serving, and self-absorbed lives. We care for none for the environment. Nor do we struggle or fight for rights. Comfort and wealth have suppressed our innate rebellious nature. We simply rely on others to lead us and show us the way. And the people who lead us know our disinterest and have seen our inaction. To appease and control us, they have progressively and stealthily replaced our social power with social comfort, now written in law. They have manipulated us so we do what is expected while living managed lives. This, we don't question, as we don't see alternatives. Nor do we know or care whether our leaders have placed us on a just path.

Is it right to be selfish? Are lives lived within governed systems based on flawed self-servicing and ill-formulated processes?

We are told greed is good as governed systems thrive on wealth creation. All our wants and needs are accommodated while consequences are dismissed and the harm caused is hidden from view. And as greed thrives on greed, we accumulate wealth that then corrupts us. This greed has led to habitat loss, reduced biodiversity, caused climate change, and created disparity that targets the vulnerable. Greed only offers limited social justice. It leads the needy and weakest into a miserable impoverished life while maximising and concentrating wealth and power to benefit the rich and powerful.

Change is difficult as our social systems are secured by laws and backed by the most powerful. When challenged, we all feel the wrath as wars are conveniently started to distract and drive public sentiment. As horrors unfold, all resistance is quashed with the disillusion of death. This is greed that can never be satisfied. It has an unquenchable thirst that tempts all it entices to attain more. This same greed has now placed all earth's resources at peril as ever-larger volumes are extracted to produce, sell, and consume more, and without feedback loops, there is no recycling. And once transported, distributed, and used, this then spreads its poison worldwide.

The Leadership Vice

Our democracy allows us to appoint the people we trust so they represent and lead us. We all think we need guidance. We seek to be saved and led to salvation, to the Promised Land. Our leaders have proclaimed they know best, knowing where we need to go. Their rhetoric makes us think they are special, and alone, they can lead us. Their charisma, ego, and appeal mesmerise us, while we forget they too can be corrupted with self-serving and selfish interests.

Leaders have a deep desire to control and hold on to power. This, however, is unattainable, as control and power can only be held momentarily, as neither is absolute or eternal. This quest then becomes a perilous journey that corrupts and consumes all who participate.

Leaders persist by manipulating the social and legal system, which they continually restructure to consolidate their power and increase their influence. Their position gives them status and privileges which they then use to sway, influence, and realise their intent. This allows them to also purposefully mislead and manipulate information with deliberate falsehoods, while broadcasting messages that sway, expand, and maximise their influence. This is how they control our fate and destiny and succeed.

To be revered and appreciated, leaders entice and reward followers with huge benefits, simply to remove the idea or hope of change. Those who rebel or resist this coercive control quickly become marginalised, forced to fight a bitter battle against the converted. This unrest provides leaders with the opportunity and reason to remove opposition and further freedoms.

As a society, we lack the will for disruptive change, always preferring the least painful path. This preference and choice is our weakness, which then makes us complicit with what occurs. This inaction corrupts us as pride does to those who lead us, as they seek to rule unchallenged with absolute power. As this occurs, a fear then grips society that removes all hope, leaving only time, forcing us to wait until this regime ages and falters.

Lust

Our sinful nature has damned us.

Sinful lust is a selfish and disordered yearning for something we don't have, don't need, but want. We all will feel such a want at least once in life. We will then intimately know lust with its desires as these dominate our minds with things that are not ours and things we are not entitled to have.

Lust can be for all things, including power, wealth, and goods. When not contained, lust can intensify, become irrational, unbridled, and can drive us crazy with needless desire. This irrational behaviour can lead to adultery, crime, and other sinful, impure acts. These desperate lustful acts only tempt us further, until we succumb completely to this evil vice. Once lust entraps us, it will slowly corrupt our mind, mentally, spiritually, and damn our soul, while enslaving our body with more wants and desires.

Lust affects many and is rife within society. Lust brings no social justice, as it favours only the rich and powerful, who then magnify their greed so they can attain and own more. This is lustful selfish greed that cares for none and devalues its opposites, chastity, and charity. This is who we are, it is our nature, and it is what we do as a society. We allow lust and greed to tempt all with the desire to attain and control more.

The richest 1% now own half of the world's wealth with the greediest 0.001% owning more than 30%. This contrasts with the poorest 20% who own only 1.4%. Both lust and greed have created this disparity which now thrives on inequality. There is no sharing with lust or greed. The rich will never share or distribute their wealth. Rather, they have enacted laws to protect them while tempting us with false hope and illusionary fairness.

This disparity exists because of the applied irrational selfishness which does not benefit people or communities. Rather it corrupts and weakens social cohesion and financial systems, often taking economies to the brink, to a tipping point where their collapse is imminent. In 2007, capitalist greed caused the largest-ever financial correction that wiped $30 trillion from accounts.

Gluttony and Consumption

Gluttony is the inordinate desire to consume more than what is required to survive.

I have never taken an accidental bite of food in my life. Each I had sought and desired. Unfortunately, however, I've taken too many bites. I am, therefore, by choice and by eating, obese.

Gluttony has already damaged me. It has corrupted me with a temptation that I cannot resist. It has also destroyed my essence by dispelling all the goodness I once had. Cast in God's image, I know I should have respected and maintained my body. I should not have dishonored it or disrespected or abused it. And yet I have allowed this vice to purposefully change and disfigure me. This has harmed and disabled me.

I know what I consume is more than I need. I also know what I eat is of low nutritional value and is bad for me. This I do because it is readily available. It is social food. It is what society prepares and provides for all. It is tasty but processed. It has high saturated fats with sugars placed there to tempt with desirable flavors, so more is consumed unnecessarily.

This is who I am. I have succumbed to the desire of this vice. I am, however, not alone. I am part of the majority who now consume food at unprecedented rates. And we are all unable to resist or abstain.

This is readily apparent in America, having 64% of its adult population and 15% of all children overweight. On average, per capita, we all are gaining weight at alarming rates. In 1977, 16% of an average US family diet was fast food, which then increased to 24% in 1987 and later in 1995, to 29%. By 2002, fast food consumption accounted for more than 40% of the average US family's food budget. This trend has made obesity a serious disease with epidemic proportions, causing the second-highest number of preventable deaths after smoking.

Greed and Consumption

A reckless thoughtlessness has allowed the wholesale conversion of the earth's natural environment into human-made capital. The pace at this happens soon will exhaust natural resources and irreparably damage the environment. This is how our society functions and how our economy is driven. Biased accounting systems and processes are used that only measure and record gains and income while dismissing the irreparable ecological damage. These disregard the accumulating costs of extraction and our excessive consumption of natural capital. As forests are cleared, soils eroded, aquifers polluted, wildlife and fisheries taken to the brink of extinction, our balance sheets show positive gains.

Easter Island's tragic and ominous tale reflects our present dilemma and predicament. This story began with the original inhabitants believing they had unlimited resources and time. They thought flora and fauna existed only for their enjoyment and use, and thereby, placed no limit on what was taken. Consumption soon improved their wellbeing and quality of life and assured prosperity, albeit for a time. Soon, however, the damage consumption caused to their environment fated their future. This tale ends in AD 1775 when Captain Cook visited this island and only found remnants of a collapsed past civilisation with its descendants eking out a marginal existence.

According to the World Commission on Environment and Development (WCED) at least 12% of the natural environment should be protected and preserved. The more conservative-minded people believe this should be increased to 25% so to stop further declines in biodiversity. With a greater area, human activity would be restricted to protect what remains, and allow the large vulnerable, and endangered carnivores to persist and adapt to a changing world. We, however, are not willing to share this planet. Our greed and our unquenchable desire to own and consume more than we need is at odds with the charity, temperance, and chastity that is required to protect the world's ecosystems with biodiversity. Without change, it is likely the Easter Island tale will soon repeat, however, on a much larger and global scale. Then it will be us who will be held to account for our foolishness.

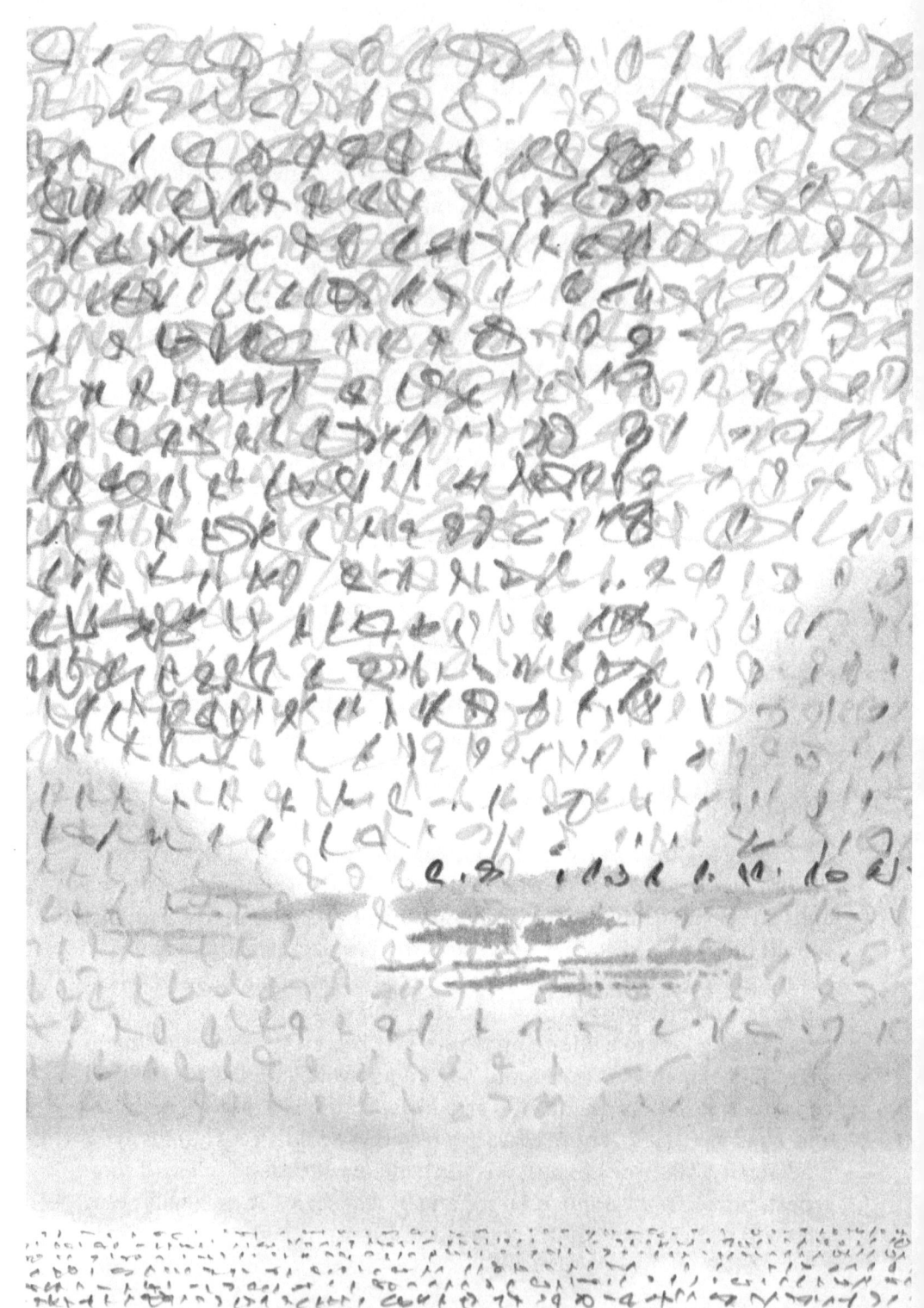

74

Greed and Corruption

Temptation with greed has the power to corrupt completely.

We all are susceptible to the temptation of greed. We all have a desire to earn, attain, and own more. This is who we are and what drives us.

Society reflects this, our imperfect human nature, our inability to balance or control our greed with abstinence or charity. Society is a product of all we are and what we have been as individuals and a community. We have devised its system and processes that compete for resources, wealth, and power. What we have created then always tempts us, beckoning us with cravings to acquire more so our desire remains unfulfilled. We may try to understand who we are and what we do by questioning ourselves, seeking to know whether we are good or evil, just or unjust, moral or immoral. We may also think those we respect are righteous, mighty, and pious, only to inevitably find they also succumb to the same vices.

Life does tempt us all with desires, including those most respected, those who lead and represent us in all industries and government. The most ambitious often reveal their true nature as they strive ruthlessly to maintain and expand their reach and empire. Pride has changed them into self-centered, selfish, and egotistical people who survive by broadcasting the failings of others through webs of deception that distract us, masking the awful truth. Those who participate help create self-serving crises that then make us all complicit. And by living within their regime we also accept their rule that ultimately traps us within their lies. No one is then free to leave or remove themselves from this reality, nor is dissension allowed. Those who try to rebel find their voice quickly drowned by mass misinformation and killed by social inaction.

We all have the means to change and improve things but rarely do. Rather, we rely on our leaders to do this as they lead us, only to find later we were misled as they amassed power and continued with the status quo. Our social inaction has allowed this. This is the awful truth. For change to occur, we must all participate. We must all join the fight against greed and the most powerful, corrupt, and autocratic, those who we had trusted most and who are still professing to lead us to their promised land.

List of Corrupted Officials
from 2000 to 2012

Politics and crime are the same thing.

From 2000 to 2012, hundreds of senior US officials were convicted while serving in government office. Wikipedia[1] has listed the following convicted officials:

Federal officials convicted of corruption offenses

2002   James Traficant; House of Representatives – Ohio; Bribery and gratuity.

2004   Frank Balance; House of Representatives – North Carolina; Mail fraud.

2006   Duke Cunningham; House of Representatives – California; Official bribery.

2009   William J Jefferson; House of Representatives – Louisiana; Official bribery.

2006   Bob Ney; House of Representatives – Ohio; Mail fraud.

Governors convicted of corruption offenses

2004   John G Rowland; Governor of Connecticut; Mail fraud.

2006   Edwin Edwards; Governor of Louisiana; Hobbs Act and mail fraud.

2011   Rod Blagojevich; Governor of Illinois; Hobbs Act and mail fraud.

2012   George Ryan; Governor of Illinois; Mail fraud.

2012   Don Siegelman; Governor of Alabama; Mail fraud and program bribery.

Cabinet members convicted of corruption offenses

2003   Dan Morales; Attorney General of Texas; Mail fraud.

2003   Meg Scott Phipps; North Carolina Commissioner of Agriculture; Hobbs Act.

---

[1]   https://en.wikipedia.org/wiki/List_of_United_States_federal_officials_convicted_of_corruption_offenses

Legislators convicted of corruption offenses

2000   Larry Bankston; Louisiana state senator; Travel Act.

2000   Frank Gigliotti; Pennsylvania state representative; Hobbs Act.

2000   Jeffrey D Johnson; Ohio state senator; Hobbs Act.

2001   Bob F Griffin; Speaker of the Missouri House of Representatives; Mail fraud and program bribery.

2002   Henry Cianfrani; Pennsylvania state senator; Mail fraud.

2003   Jefferson Marion Long, Jr; South Carolina state representative; Hobbs Act.

2003   John A Lynch, Jr; New Jersey state representative; Mail fraud.

2005   J Chris Newton; Tennessee state representative; Hobbs Act and program bribery.

2006   Michael P Decker; North Carolina state representative; Hobbs Act and mail fraud.

2006   Roscoe Dixon; Tennessee state senator; Hobbs Act and program bribery.

2007   James B Black; Speaker of the North Carolina House of Representatives; Program bribery.

2007   Kathryn I Bowers; Tennessee state senator; Program bribery.

2007   Thomas L Bromwell; Maryland state senator; RICO.

2007   Ward Crutchfield; Tennessee state senator; Program bribery.

2007   Pete Kott; Speaker of the Alaska House of Representatives; Hobbs Act, mail fraud, and program bribery.

2007   Ernie Newton; Connecticut state senator; Mail fraud.

2007   Charles W Walker, Sr; Georgia Senate majority leader; Mail fraud.

2008   John A Celona; Rhode Island state senator; Mail fraud.

2008   Gerard M Martineau; Rhode Island House majority leader; Mail fraud.

2009   Thomas T Anderson; Alaska state representative; Hobbs Act.

2009   John Cowdery; Alaska state senator; Program bribery.

2009   John Ford; Tennessee state senator; Wire fraud and program bribery.

2009   Beverly Masek; Alaska state representative; Travel Act.

2010   Joseph Coniglio; New Jersey state senator; Hobbs Act and mail fraud.

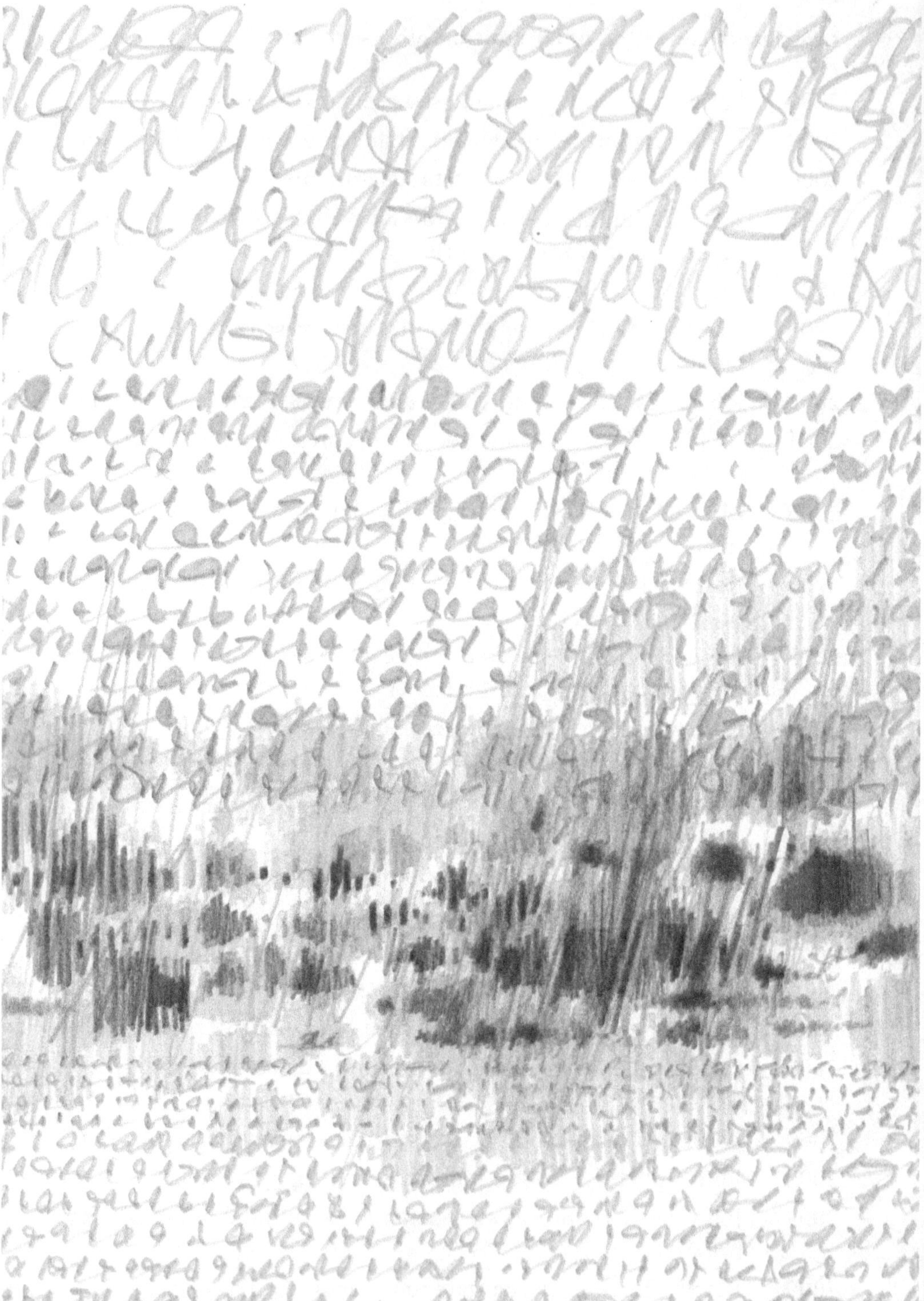

2010   Anthony Seminerio; New York state representative; Mail fraud

2010   Dianne Wilkerson; Massachusetts state senator; Hobbs Act.

2011   Wayne R Bryant; New Jersey state senator; Mail fraud and program bribery.

2011   Salvatore DiMasi; Speaker of the Massachusetts House of Representatives; Hobbs Act and mail fraud.

2011   Vince Fumo; Pennsylvania state senator; Mail fraud.

2011   Efrain Gonzalez; New York state senator; Mail fraud.

2011   Phil Hamilton; Virginia state representative; Hobbs Act and program bribery.

2011   Vic Kohring; Alaska state representative; Hobbs Act and program bribery.

2011   Suzanne L Schmitz; Alabama state representative; Mail fraud and program bribery.

2011   Dan R Tonkovich; West Virginia Senate President; Hobbs Act.

2011   Daniel Van Pelt; New Jersey state representative; Hobbs Act and program bribery.

2012   Carl Kruger; New York state senator; Mail fraud and Travel Act.

2012   Mike Morgan; Oklahoma state senator; Program bribery.

2012   Terry Spicer; Alabama state representative; Program bribery.

Local officials convicted of federal corruption offenses

2001   Milton Milan; Mayor of Camden, New Jersey; RICO.

2003   Jerome P Genova; Mayor of Calumet City, Illinois; Mail fraud, program bribery, and RICO.

2004   Buddy Cianci; Mayor of Providence, Rhode Island; RICO.

2004   Eddie Alexander Long; Mayor of Smithers, West Virginia; Mail fraud.

2004   Joseph J Santopietro; Mayor of Waterbury, Connecticut; Program bribery.

2005   Betty Loren-Maltese; Town President of Cicero, Illinois; Mail fraud and RICO.

2007	Joseph Ganim; Mayor of Bridgeport, Connecticut; Hobbs Act, mail fraud, program bribery, and RICO.
2007	Theodore LeBlanc; Mayor of Norristown, Pennsylvania; Mail fraud and program bribery.
2007	Emmanuel Onunwor; Mayor of East Cleveland, Ohio; RICO.
2007	Anthony Russo; Mayor of Hoboken, New Jersey; Mail fraud.
2008	Samuel Rivera; Mayor of Passaic, New Jersey; Hobbs Act.
2008	Steven Eugene Russo; Mayor of Orange Beach, Alabama; Mail fraud.
2009	Eddie Price III; Mayor of Mandeville, Louisiana; Mail fraud.
2010	Peter Cammarano; Mayor of Hoboken, New Jersey; Hobbs Act.
2010	David Delle Donna; Mayor of Guttenberg, New Jersey; Hobbs Act.
2010	Sharpe James; Mayor of Newark, New Jersey; Mail fraud and program bribery.
2011	Yvonne A Dockery; Mayor of Garland, Arkansas; Mail fraud.
2011	Dennis Elwell; Mayor of Secaucus, New Jersey; Program bribery.
2011	Larry Langford; Mayor of Birmingham, Alabama; Mail and wire fraud and program bribery.
2011	Gerald McCann; Mayor of Jersey City, New Jersey.
2011	Maurice B Brown; Mayor of White Castle, Louisiana; Mail fraud, RICO, and Travel Act.
2012	John Pomierski; Mayor of Upland, California.
2012	David Silva; Mayor of Cudahy, California.

City council members convicted of corruption offenses

2000	Virgil Jones; Chicago Alderman; Hobbs Act.
2001	Percy Giles; Chicago Alderman; Hobbs Act, mail fraud, and RICO.
2001	Robert Leslie Williams; City Council of Jackson, Mississippi; Hobbs Act and program bribery.
2004	Andrew K Mirikitani; Honolulu City Council; Program bribery.
2005	Robert Burke; Alderman of Holly Springs, Mississippi; Hobbs Act and Travel Act.

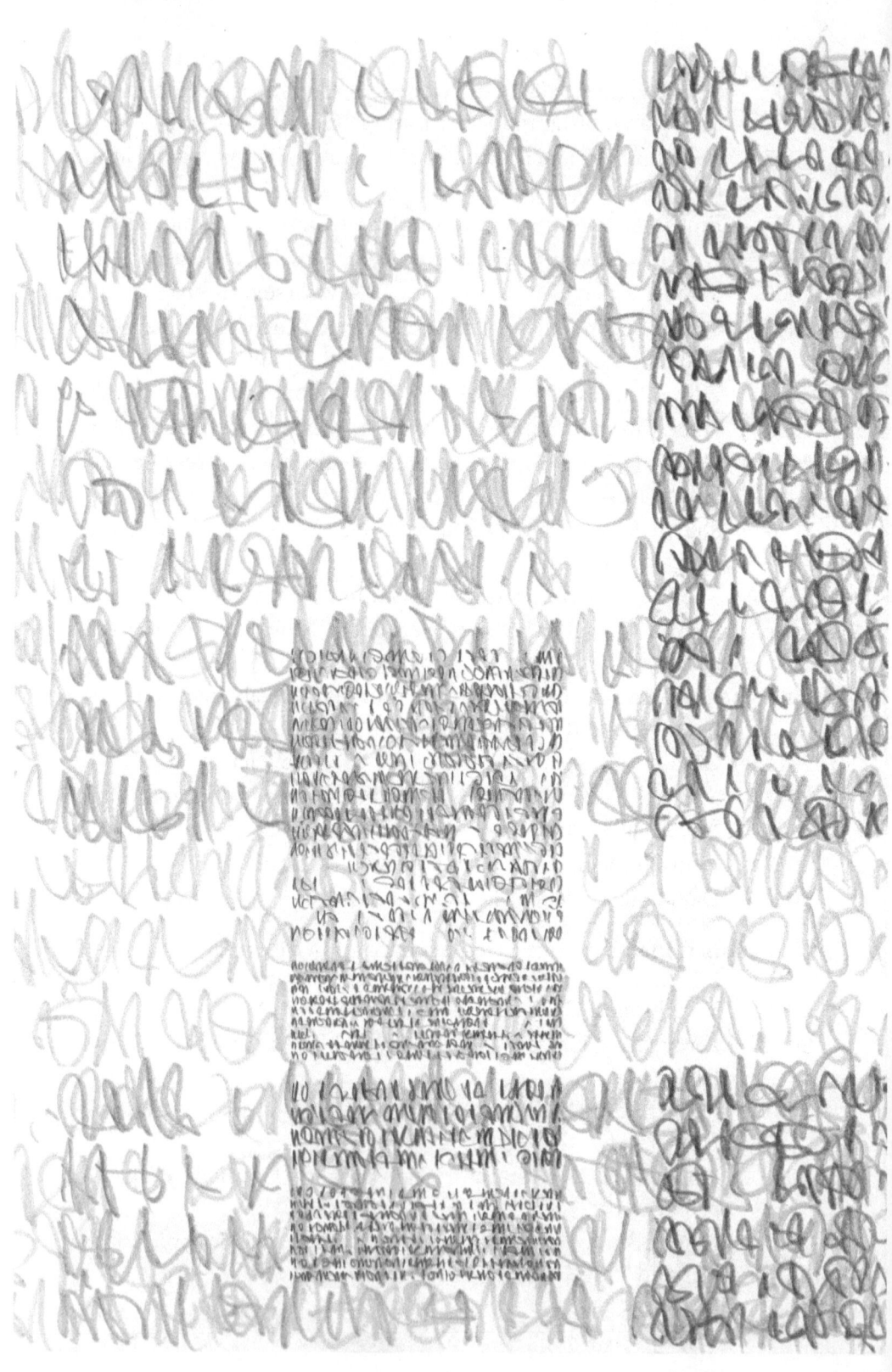

2005	Gwendolyn Cheek Hedgepeth; Richmond City Council; Hobbs Act and mail fraud.
2005	Angel Rodriguez; New York City Council; Hobbs Act.
2006	Thomas Flaherty; Jersey City Council; Hobbs Act.
2006	Jack Foster; Alderman of Pine Bluff, Arkansas; Hobbs Act.
2007	Michael D'Amico; City Councilor of Quincy, Massachusetts; Hobbs Act.
2007	Oliver Thomas; New Orleans City Council; Program bribery.
2008	Ed Jew; San Francisco Board of Supervisors; Mail fraud, Hobbs Act, and program bribery.
2008	Raymond J O'Grady; Township Committeeman of Middletown, New Jersey; Hobbs Act and program bribery.
2008	Michael Orsburn; Trustee of Keener Township in Jasper County, Indiana; Mail fraud.
2009	Ralph Inzunza; San Diego City Council; Hobbs Act and mail fraud.
2009	Miguel Martinez; New York City Council; Mail fraud.
2009	Michael Zucchet; San Diego City Council; Hobbs Act and mail fraud.
2010	Isaac Carothers; Chicago Alderman.
2010	Monica Conyers; Detroit City Council; Program bribery.
2010	Chuck Turner; Boston City Council; Hobbs Act.
2010	Edward Vrdolyak; Chicago Alderman; Mail and wire fraud.
2011	Arthur Gilmore, Jr; Monroe City Council; Hobbs Act and RICO.
2011	John J Hamilton, Jr; Councilman of Asbury Park, New Jersey; Hobbs Act and program bribery.
2011	Robert E Stevens; Monroe City Council; Hobbs Act and RICO.
2012	William Carothers; Chicago Alderman; Hobbs Act.
2012	Fred Hubbard; Chicago Alderman; Program bribery.
2012	Marian Humes; Chicago Alderman
2012	Perry Hutchinson; Chicago Alderman.
2012	Joseph Jambroni; Chicago Alderman.
2012	Clifford Kelley; Chicago Alderman.

2012	Tyrone Kenner; Chicago Alderman
2012	John Madryzk; Chicago Alderman.
2012	Joseph Martinez; Chicago Alderman.
2012	Joseph Potempa; Chicago Alderman.
2012	Fred Roti; Chicago Alderman; Hobbs Act and RICO.
2012	Larry Seabrook; New York City Councilman; Mail and wire fraud.
2012	Edward Scholl; Chicago Alderman.
2012	Arenda Troutman; Chicago Alderman; Mail fraud.
2012	Stanley Zydlo; Chicago Alderman.

County executives and commissioners

2002	Robert C Janiszewski; County Executive of Hudson County, New Jersey; Hobbs Act.
2003	James W Treffinger; County Executive of Essex County, New Jersey; Mail fraud.
2007	Erin Kenny; Commissioner of Clark County, Nevada; Wire fraud.
2009	Mary Kincaid-Chauncey; Commissioner of Clark County, Nevada; Hobbs Act and wire fraud.
2009	Lance Malone; Commissioner of Clark County, Nevada; RICO.
2010	Greg Skrepenak; Luzerne County Board of Commissioners; Program bribery.
2011	Jack B Johnson; County Executive of Prince George's County, Maryland.
2012	Jimmy Dimora; Commissioner of Cuyahoga County, Ohio; RICO.

Sloth

Sloth is the absence of self-respect and self-love.

At one time or another, we will be found guilty of being lazy. Modern life with its technology has allowed this. We all have the means to indulge ourselves with slothful desires while forgoing physical activity and leading sedentary lives.

The inactivity of sloth changes people. It changes who we are, what we do, and who we become. This brings on an apathetic listlessness that replaces joy and contentment with depression and melancholy that overwhelms us, soon finding we lose our ability to care for others and ourselves. This is when we desperately need help.

As joy vanishes and happiness disappears a bitterness sets in. All contentment from life then also slips away. Left untreated, this consumes us, our heart conditioning us within inactivity. This then separates us so we become isolated, losing our ability to relate to others and the realities of life. Devoid of social interaction, life then also loses meaning and becomes an ordeal that focuses solely on persevering through the next hours and day.

The vice of sloth can affect us all. Our self-serving nature provides ample reason to laze and not work or help others. And if this becomes our mind-set, this will then also influence everything else we do, including how we live. And by allowing sloth to become us, we then selfishly dismiss and disregard everyone and everything that once matter. All we once valued, including our family and friends, then will disappear. And by not caring or doing what is good or right, we then also damn ourselves.

Spiritual Sin

Evil soon learned how to hide in plain sight.

In the distant past, evil was contained when the sinful, stained individuals were removed and separated from the community. These stained souls had to be kept at a safe distance so the community was protected from the evil they carried and emanated. Ostracised, these individuals then lived solitary, isolated lives. They were given refuge in temples while forced to repent with prayer to atone for the evil they had within.

Today these same stained souls now live freely among us, no longer needing to isolate or repent. And with the opportunities they are given, they integrate themselves into society while pursuing their malevolent intent. They have used their cunning ability to progress rapidly through hierarchical structures, in every organisation, institution, and government, taking positions as religious ministers, priests, professed saviours, teachers, trainers, and carers. They distinguish themselves with toil while disguising their true nature and intent. And with an unholy ability, they entice many with promises of wealth, power, and privilege. This they do to strengthen and expand their network and reach, and to realise their darkest desires. These souls are corrupt, sinful, stained, and the servants of evil. Evil has especially chosen places of worship so to desecrate the sacred, corrupt the innocent, and damn the faithful. Many stained individuals have risen through ranks to occupy the most prominent prestigious positions while spreading their sinful sloth that undermines all spiritual endeavours. All that was once sacred is now defiled. All religious conviction, commitment, and servitude, along with social values of chastity, temperance, charity, diligence, forgiveness, gratitude, and humility are now corrupted. All of these have been replaced with sinful deeds, as revealed by the 2004 John Jay Report[2]. This report revealed 10,667 pending allegations against 4,392 high-ranking priests and clergy who had sexually abused minors. Decades later, by 2019, 1,700 of the accused were still not charged or prosecuted and likely never be held to account for the evil they had unleashed.

---

[2]   https://en.wikipedia.org/wiki/John_Jay_Report

Evil Contagion

Social apathy with spiritual sloth has enabled an evil contagion to spread, corrupting souls and desecrating our most sacred places. This has dawned a new darkened forsaken reality that keeps corrupting innocence and dismays the faithful with its evil spread.

Good is no longer welcomed here!

Evil has manipulated our minds and society. It has changed our destiny, purposefully and intentionally diverting us away from the righteous path.

We are all to blame. Our ignorance together with our selfish self-serving pride has been used to deceive the righteous and corrupt society from within. This has now spread like an unstoppable contagion.

No one sees or understands what occurs or cares about how people suffer. What occurs is behind closed doors, submerged below daily life, hidden from view to be later forgotten, placed deep in our subconsciousness so it never resurfaces or is reconciled. This is the invisible anguish that brings mental disease that grips and churns minds, sowing its evil seeds so these grow, expand, evolve, and strengthen. There is no remedy or cure for how this then progressively corrupts our innocence, destroys our lives, and consumes us. Evil with this contagious spread is winning its war.

This I know because I am damned. My past self had allowed darkness to envelop and stain me. When evil entered, I became a servant to the cause and was driven to corrupt and destroy all I could. I remembered preaching, declaring to be just, pious, and righteous while gathering, harvesting, and consuming innocent souls. This was my past when I was corrupt, sick, and needy with unfulfilled unholy desires. The evil that controlled me then, I still have within. It continuously spreads its seed of contagion where it can, seeking to again expand, flourish, and continue with its evil intentions on earth.

Wrath through Time

The fight between good and evil will never end. War is coming.

For eternity, humanity has fought with itself. History is marred with many recorded conflicts and wars, all revealing our dormant hidden vengeful nature. It has recorded who we are and what we are capable of with an eternal unending struggle. This, we all have inherited, along with ancient horrid memories of violence, trauma, and atrocities. This is the curse we all carry deep within our subconsciousness.

We all relate to war and violence. This had defined us as a race and humanity. Some ancient fight-flight physiological response morphed to become our fighting spirit, our nature, one that brings forth anger and war. This helped us persevere through hard times and survive great perils. Now no longer needing this, try as we might, we cannot erase this. All we can do is manage and control this.

We fool ourselves if we think we are above anger or war. Our civil governed society has only temporarily removed the need to fight and survive. We still carry within a deep-seated fear that one day soon evil will arise within us and take us to where we don't want to go.

Are you aware of the fragility of peace? Do you not see war coming?

Confronting what we have within us is hard. We feel evil when we see atrocities unfolding before us. We question, how can this happen? As we continue to watch, we feel this exposure change and desensitise us, soon to find the horrid becomes familiar, normal, and necessary. This is when evil touches us and we succumb to it. It then proceeds to corrupt and damn us. In war, this occurs when the killing starts. This evil envelopes soldiers, as darkness does to nightfall. It temporarily hardens and corrupts them, substituting all thoughts and ambitions with a contagious unyielding and uncompromising hatred. This transforms them into unremorseful, unrepentant, desensitised, and damned souls that then commence feeding on death. With evil inside, they travel at lightning speed with a ferocity that harms and destroys all they touch. They become unstoppable, devastated individuals, combatants that partake in all the horrors of battle. When the war ends and this evil dissipates, they soon forget this madness, only to be reminded later as veterans of what they did to survive.

Sinful Participation

I took my mind back to relive my past. I then regressed some 5,000 years only to find some deep darkness of continuing despair. There, I began to relive many sinful incarnations. Soon, I understood who I was and how I had stained my soul. I found myself as female mostly, living in a man's world. I was true to evil, I had become its dutiful servant, causing willful pain, suffering, and harm, to devastate all I could. I found myself reincarnating every third generation or so, countless times. When I found myself in battle, I did not seek glory but death. Some of the many historical conflicts and wars I found myself participating in were:

- AD 1914 – World War 1 – with its 16m (million) deaths.
- AD 1803 – Napoleonic Wars – with its 7m deaths.
- AD 1775 – American Revolutionary War – with its 37,324 deaths.
- AD 1701 – War of the Spanish Succession – with its 1.2m deaths.
- AD 1635 – Franco-Spanish War (1635–59) – with its 200,000 deaths.
- AD 1585 – Anglo-Spanish War (1585–1604) – with its 138,285 deaths.
- AD 1519 – Spanish versus the Aztec Empire – with its 2.3m deaths.
- AD 1455 – Wars of the Roses – with its 50,000 deaths.
- AD 1337 – Hundred Years' War – with its 3.3m deaths.
- AD 1208 – Albigensian Crusade – with its 1m deaths.
- AD 1095 – Crusades – with its 3m deaths.
- AD 993 – Goryeo-Khitan Wars – with its 90,000 deaths.
- AD 711 – Reconquista – with its 10m deaths.
- AD 629 – Arab-Byzantine Wars – with its 130,000 deaths.
- AD 534 – Moorish Wars – with its 5m deaths.
- AD 376 – Gothic War – with its 40,000 deaths.
- AD 269 – Gothic War – with its 320,000 deaths.
- AD 132 – Bar Kokhba Revolt – with its 580,000 deaths.
- AD 60 – Iceni Revolt – with its 150,000 deaths.
- 58 BC – Gallic Wars – with its 1m deaths.
- 149 BC – Third Punic War – with its 250,000 deaths.
- 264 BC – First Punic War – with its 400,000 deaths.
- 343 BC – Samnite Wars – with its 33,500 deaths.
- 549 BC – Conquests of Cyrus the Great – with its 100,000 deaths.

Envy - Hatred and Crime

Envy of the devil brought death to the world. ~ Wisdom 2:24

Envy, like lust and greed, can be a damning vice. Envy often tempts with an intense jealously that persuades, so we succumb to desires and take what is not ours. Envy veers us off course; with it, we lose sight of what is right and corrupt ourselves. This is humanly familiar, we all have experienced some form of this, as perpetrators, victims, or both.

Our human nature has a deep-seated envious desire that can arise unexpectedly, unintentionally, and can be called at will. And when it comes, it does so with malicious jealousy that quickly fills our minds, seeking to deprive others of status and property. This is when we corrupt ourselves as we start dwelling on others' lives and affairs. By not understanding why some succeed and we don't, we start believing there is no justice and are persuaded to seek restitution. We then take what is not ours, including property, success, status, and ultimately life. This only harms and produces no contentment, or satisfaction, and nor does it justifiably right some past wrong. This false logic corrupts our minds with some arrogant, uncontrollable, envious jealously that rouses every thought with feelings of entitlement.

Envy does have deadly consequences. This led Cain to murder his brother Abel. Today the daily news broadcast its deadly crime statistics, rife with envious consequences. The United States has the highest, with an average of 6.64 murders per 100,000 people each year.

Envy has always tempted humanity with some desire and evil intent. We all know what occurs when we succumb. We have seen this and experienced this. This is a malicious vice that is hard to ignore, dismiss, resist, and overcome as it truly entices, to then corrupt and damn. This vice is the curse that evil placed on us to enslave us to its will.

Pride - Base of Power

Careful! Your pride might enslave you.

Only pride weighs down the soul more than any other vice. Pride is the original and most sinful vice of all. It can unleash utmost evil.

Pride is directly linked to the devil. It had made the devil. It is the devil's prominent trait and has laid the foundation for all other vices.

As a society, we encourage pride. We all are susceptible to feelings of pride as it is essential to have self-respect which is required for good leadership. Left unchecked, however, it can lead to irrational behaviour, focused self-adoration, and power quests. With pride seeding and growing in our minds, we begin thinking we are better, superior, and more important than any other person. Such egotistical self-admiration allows us to discard all other concerns or cares, allowing us also to overlook our faults and all the wrong we do.

Blinded, unable to see the wrongs we do, our minds are then filled with unjust desires, urges, wants, and whims. When challenged, our mind turns to deceit and vengeance that fuels an emerging maliciousness. This seeds a meanness inside that nourished our selfish thoughts with irrational beliefs and thoughts of entitlement. A malevolent intent then begins to formulate in our minds that consume all remaining logic and goodness. Rapid intervention is required and necessary to stop this from taking us to its extreme and irrevocably changing us. Adolf Hitler personified this unbridled pride. It took him on a brief meteoric rise, only to be stopped by the end of WW2 and his suicide in 1945.

Today excessive indulgent pride is readily apparent and evident throughout the world. All self-appointed dictators personify pride and still rule unchallenged in countries such as Afghanistan, Algeria, Angola, Azerbaijan, Bahrain, Belarus, Brunei, Burundi, Cambodia, Cameroon, Central African Republic, Chad, China, the Democratic Republic of the Congo, Republic of the Congo (Brazzaville), Cuba, Djibouti, Egypt, Equatorial Guinea, Eritrea, Ethiopia, Gabon, Iran, Iraq, Kazakhstan, Laos, Libya, Myanmar, Mauritania, Nicaragua, North Korea, Oman, Qatar, Russia, Rwanda, Saudi Arabia, Somalia, South Sudan, Sudan, Swaziland (Eswatini), Syria, Tajikistan, Thailand, Turkey, Turkmenistan, Uganda, United Arab Emirates, Uzbekistan, Venezuela, Vietnam, Western Sahara, and Yemen.

The Gift of Free Will

Free will is a divine gift given to us all. This gift gives us choice and enables us to decide who we are, who we become, and how we live our lives. We can choose to be active, reactive, responsive, and/or inactive. We can also choose to be just or unjust, moral, or corrupt.

This gift, which is supposed to lead us to our destiny, is, however, also a curse. To reach our destiny, we are required to stay on course, on the just path, and not divert or be bad.

What we decide, choose, and do is, therefore, important. We alone become responsible and accountable for what occurs. This is why we must learn to rein in and control our selfish and self-serving pride with corrupt thoughts so these don't become acts that cause harm and accrue karmic debt. We must be mindful of what we do as we will need to live with the repercussions and consequences of our actions and deeds.

We progress and evolve by living just. We gain knowledge, worth, a benevolent heart, intellect, and empathy, all that we retain through life as positive energy and karmic capital. By living just, we also contribute to the expanding global consciousness and well-being. This we must do to reach our destiny.

What we choose as individuals reflects within our society. What we decide is what society does. Therefore, what we do has social, national, and global consequences that do not diminish, fade, or disappear but accrue as either social karmic debt or capital. This is why everything we do matters. Whether we contribute, participate, or not, we, nevertheless and inadvertently, are part of a social system. We all become complicit with what occurs and what society does. If this system causes harm, we become part of the problem. Not voicing our concerns and failing to provide valid solutions or remedies is, thereby, inexcusable, as this only reveals our uncaring nature that only underlies an overall indifference to what occurs. We, thereby, cannot ignore what is happening.

We should all know our society is heading to a precipice. Doomsayers proclaim the next-world mass extinction is nigh. And if we were fortunate to survive, we would then have to live with all the combined consequences of all our actions and inactions.

Karmic Debt

Karma is an enigma. It is a form of intertwined emotional/metaphysical energy that is ruled by vindication. It has the power not only to influence but also to hold people and places to account. It exists to ensure order and cosmic balance are maintained; this it does by ensuring rampant evil is controlled and quelled before it completely decimates and consumes all life that exists. It manifests only when needed. And when it comes, it does so to punish perpetrators while remembering victims and ensuring their suffering was not in vain.

Karmic debt is accrued when divergence occurs from the divine plan and just path. This separates us from the eternal divine by doing evil. Then, when all the wrongs we have done can no longer be dismissed and we persist, karma will intervene. It will come to control, seeking out and punishing corrupt souls. It will then remain, overseeing what occurs, often for generations, until all bad that has occurred is reconciled and evil is quelled.

Karma exists here with us. Everything we do, have done, every action, all the lives we had lived, all we had contributed and amounted to, is either karmic capital or debt. All the good is karmic capital, which will help us reach our destiny. All our sins and misdeeds becomes the debt we carry until it is reconciled.

Good deeds sowed ripely will bring success and happiness, while the debt we owe will weigh heavily on us, and bring us pain, misery, and misfortune. Debt is, however, unlike capital. It is finite. Beyond some point and amount, it must be reconciled and repaid to maintain the cosmic order and balance. It has an end date. This is when all the maliciousness and evil we had done will be held to account. This is when we, the souls that are corrupted and stained with evil, will be forced to repay and reconcile what we had done. Karma will ensure this occurs. It will intervene to oversee and control all that occurs until universal equilibrium is again restored between good and evil.

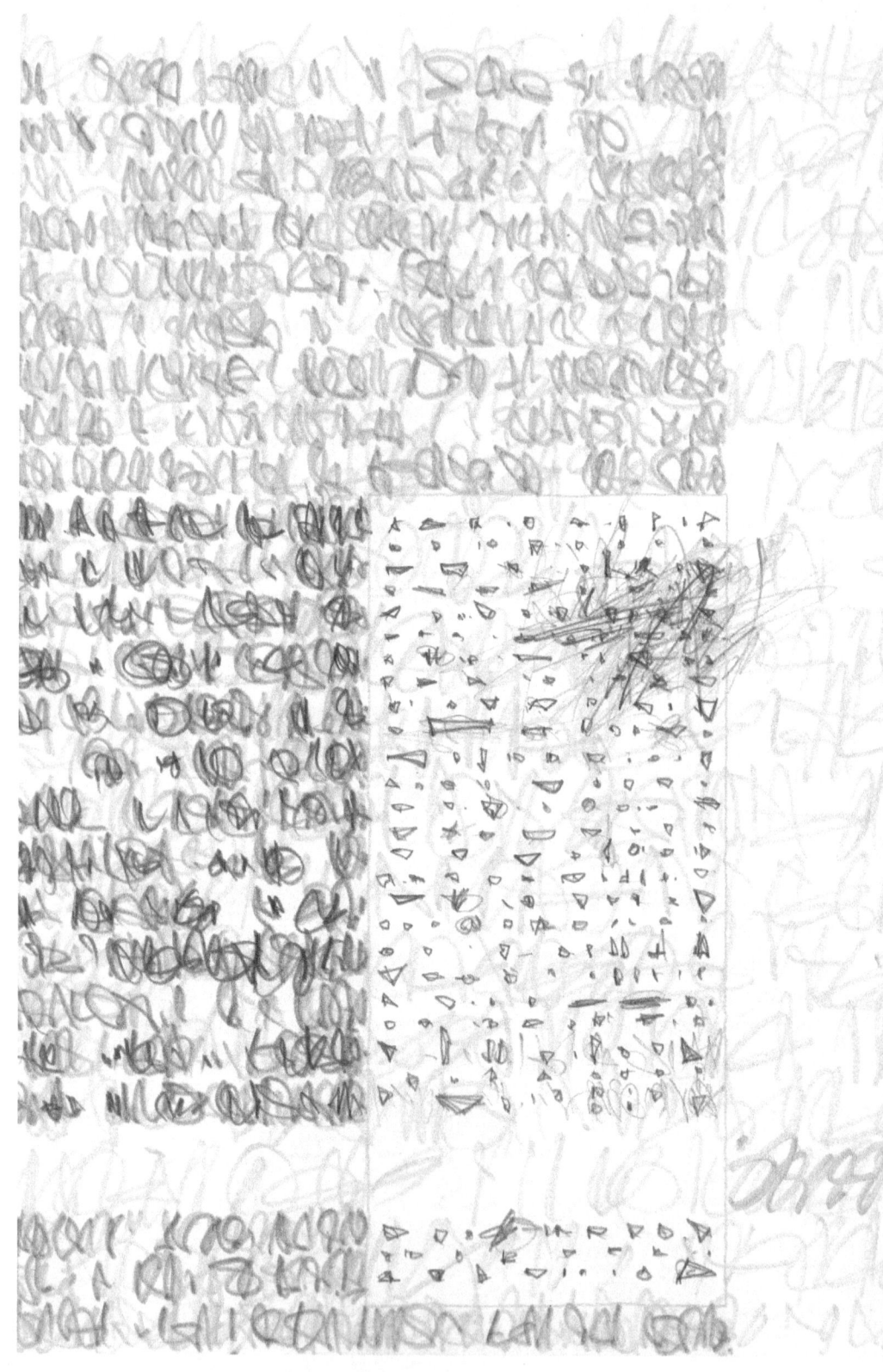

Our Karmic Debt

There exist an eternal dualist tension between good and evil. Each is supremely powerful. Each has the power and means to cancel the other, but neither does. Each needs the other to exist, being an opposite that holds together this plane as a fragile whole.

Karma reacts when evil tries to dominate. This it does to ensure evil is sufficiently contained so it does not devastate completely. Karma will not dispel evil nor remove it completely or eliminate it. It can only defeat it, subdue it, so it dissipates and withdraws back into its darkness. Defeated and as it waits to reemerge, it will continue with its business, trying to enter people's hearts by tempting susceptible souls with ungodly desires and vices.

Evil is here, it is with us! It is here to unleash its intent on us.

We feel evil when we succumb to temptation. This is also when we accrued karmic debt. This we do as individuals and as a society of people. I know this. I have seen this. Karma, my keeper, has given me the ability to see this. I see how debt accrues and the balance rapidly mounts into arrears. This is all the misery and pain we had unleashed on each other and on this world. This we have done as individuals and society, causing losses and harm, zero-sum outcomes, with no one ever benefiting.

As a global society, we have all become complicit. We allow the vulnerable to be harmed and the environment to be irreparably damaged. We do this while knowing this is diminishing future opportunities, not just for humanity but for every other living thing on this planet. We also know what has already been done cannot easily be undone or reconciled. We had allowed this to occur as we fail to understand the difference between right and wrong. We see no distinction. Bad continues as we benefit, mounting our gains. We think others will do what's right and save us but we are mistaken. Globalisation has already linked and tied all our fates together. There are no others. All people, all nations, and countries are already one. We all participate, are complicit, and equally responsible, accountable, and liable for all that occurs and will eventuate. In the end, we all will be forced to reconcile this. This is our accrued global karmic debt that will soon be called due.

The Unforgiven

I see my image reflected from the watery surface. I notice a dark cloud encroaching my shadow to slowly envelope the pond, darkening my surroundings.

Is this an ominous sign, a warning of what is to come?

I have tried to reconcile my past while I live this sentenced life. I wished I could be freed but know this sentence will take me to my death. There will be no shortcuts or reprieve for what I must endure. Nor can I negotiate or change this. Karma has set this in stone. This is the life I must live.

Karma is here with me now. I feel it. It follows me. It oversees everything I do, ensuring each day I suffer for what I had done. I am the unforgiven.

Here, I live a dual existence. I am forced to be just and righteous while having an immoral and evil heart. I try to do right, but my nature often rebels and does wrong. I struggle with this evil as it tempts me with desires to sin. I need to continually maneuver past this to remain good.

I have tried to atone for all the bad I had done. I have also tried to reconcile all the consequences of my past misdeed. I, however, still fail. I cannot do what is right or expected. All my previous prejudices remain and exist within me, always tempting and persuading me to do wrong. My mind is always filled with discriminating evil thoughts. I think everyone is inferior, subordinate, or an enemy. This, I know, I must stop. I must learn to purge and dispel these thoughts before they become reality. Evil, however, keeps tempting me, every second of every day. It tempts me to participate, and join its perpetual fight with goodness. Often I cannot stop what I do and fear my gestures will become horrible and terrible actions. Evil seeks to cause harm to people and communities, decreeing it will spare none. This I feel as palpable anger and resentment raging within me, coaxing me to participate. Often I see this manifest into reality as the disgruntled who heed this call, allow their vengeance to cause harm, and kill outright. I see how this evil tempts with its persuasion, turning brother against brother. This I must resist. I must not succumb to this evil as I don't want to be damned for eternity. I want to be saved.

Balance and Duality

With creation, there must be destruction. With light, darkness, and life, there must be death.

Everything has an opposite. White has black. Good has evil. This is the law of polarity. This also exists with a duality that keeps the whole in balance. This is the law of correspondence.

At the beginning of creation, everything manifested into existence together, simultaneously. Everything came from one origin, separating into distinct parts, yet inextricably linked. The polarity and duality that exists hold the whole together. It has created tension with opposites that prevent its collapse and return to its origin. It is this tension that has given life to matter, allowing it to exist and persist.

Opposites coexist, as these prevent the absolute power of one from collapsing into itself and ending this reality.

Life has been defined and ruled by the duality that exists. This has allowed life to be good and bad. As one dominates or climaxes, its opposite will quell its surge, stopping the extreme from occurring, to again restore balance. This ensures ebbs and flows are always short-lived.

We all know this occurs. We have heard miracles from God and its opposite, evil incarnate manifest here on earth, only for providence to intervene, to restore and maintain balance.

We are all affected by this dichotomy with duality. It influences everything we do, who we are, and how we live as individuals and as a society. This becomes evident when we consider how successful people fail in life, how educated people fail to understand logic, how lonesome people can live within crowded cities, and how the rich and powerful morally bankrupt themselves.

By knowing and understanding the differences between right and wrong, we should also know how life should be lived. Despite this, we often and purposefully do what we shouldn't. We succumb to vices, do wrong, and without reason, often veer off the just path. Despite this and what we might think or intend to do, this duality and dichotomy will forever persist and influence our lives.

The Univeral Laws

Life on earth is balanced perfectly by natural laws. These are the universal laws that define all that exists, including how life should be lived on this plane. These are:

- The law of divine oneness – everything is connected to everything else.
- The law of action – everything has or will soon manifest.
- The law of cause and effect – we reap what we sow.
- The law of compensation – actions and deeds will accrue either as karmic capital or debt.
- The law of attraction – positive attracts the negative and the negative, the positive.
- The law of gestation – seeded ideas will germinate and then manifest into reality with divine timing.
- The law of correspondence – the duality that exists between opposites.
- The law of relativity – no matter how bad a situation is, there is always worse.
- The law of polarity – everything has an opposite.
- The law of mental vibrations – we all can suppress and transform undesirable thoughts with mental concentration.
- The law of vibration – everything moves in a certain motion.
- The law of rhythm – everything moves by seasons, cycles, stages of development, and patterns.
- The law of gender – everything has a masculine and feminine side, yin and yang, this is the basis of all creation.
- The law of belief – all beliefs soon manifest into reality.
- The law of perpetual transmutation of energy – we have the power to change conditions if we choose to do so.

These laws have established balance and equilibrium on this plane. And if an imbalance does occur by good or evil dominating, these laws will manifest their redeeming forces, to restore balance.

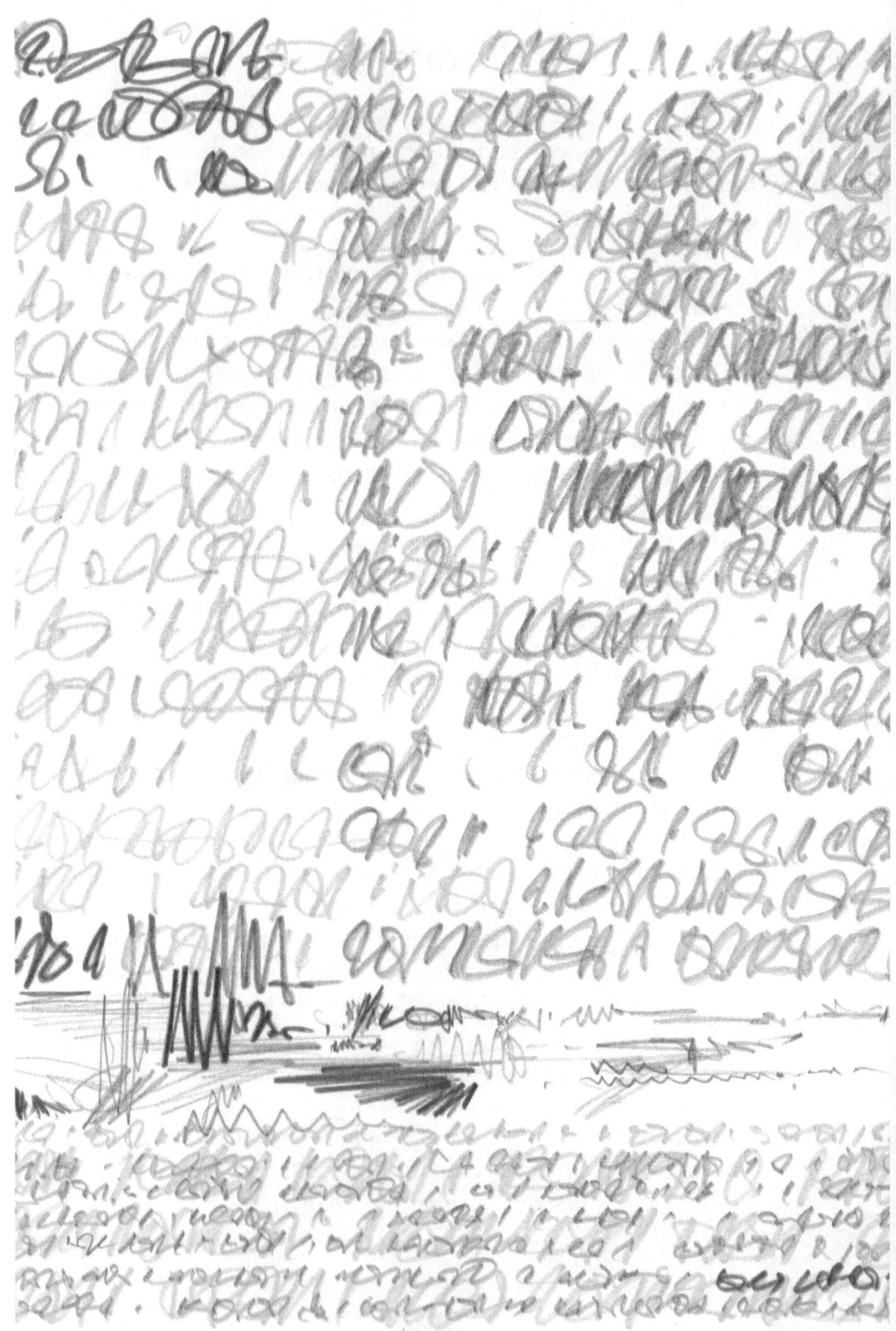

Free Will

The divine gift of free will is a blessing and curse. The blessing is the freedom afforded to us. We are all free to choose, set our life path, and thereby, also determine our fate. The curse of freedom is its accountability, the long-lasting eternal consequences of the choices we make.

The fate of humanity hangs in balance.

Only the just and righteous can reach enlightenment. This, however, is difficult and near impossible for us mortals. Life has a slippery inclination that is placed here to stymie progress and corrupt our innocence with temptation and desires to sin.

We may think we alone decide and set our path, choosing which journey we take in life. But by thinking this, we forget how corruptible human nature is, as it is forever influenced by temptation. Freedom with temptation breeds selfishness that then leads to sinful life choices that are hard to dismiss or overcome.

There is no true freedom or choice, as wrongful, sinful choices and decisions do have consequences and create outcomes that will need to be reconciled. Only karma keeps tally of what we do and the debt we accrue. We will only know when we are either sentenced for the bad we had done or reach enlightenment for being just and righteous.

I had accrued substantial karmic debt that sentenced me. My bad choices and misdeeds had set my fate. I had the freedom to act differently and change, and reconcile the bad I had done, but inadvertently, I chose to stain myself by consistently being bad and doing evil. I did this intentionally, simply not to be good. Nor would I stop or repent or atone for all the harm I had caused. And by not wanting to change, karma intervened and sentenced me. Free will and choice had damned me.

Life with Dilemma

I was recycled back into this reality. I was placed here, on this physical plane, to atone for my sins and redeem myself. Karma gave me this life as punishment.

I was in denial during my youth and adolescence. I was in a self-induced primal, youthful state of ingenuousness immaturity. I was deceitful, treacherous, and foolish. I had to wait until I sufficiently matured to gain some clarity in thought. For many years, I struggled, disillusioned with life. My youth held me back. It filled me with false hopes of entitlement that corrupted my mind.

The fog that clouded my youthful mind only lifted when I had matured. I then began rationalising and quickly learned the truth. I had finally transcended past youthful adolescent thoughts of entitlement and future reprieve. I began to understand the full extent of my dilemma. I was not innocent. I deserved this lifelong sentence. This, my fate, I had to accept. All my past misdeeds and the misery I had caused had damned me. I then also knew there would be no reprieve for me.

Life has since taught me to be determined in thought and ready to face all that lies ahead of me. This, I must do so I can endure this sentence to its end. I had finally understood my purpose in life. I now know in this life, I must stay on the just path. I must seek redemption. I must redeem myself to be forgiven. Karma has given me this, the opportunity to dispel the evil I carry within, repair my corrupted soul, and regain some goodness.

I have since learned to live with the sentence given to me. All I do now is endure this miserable existence without again succumbing to evil. And by resigning to this fate, I am also determined, knowing I will never again succumb to temptation. I now know what is right, and as I stay on course, I simply endure what is and what is still to come.

Acceptance

It is not about being good or evil; rather, it is about acknowledging and accepting past wrongs and reconciling these.

It is unfair and unjust that we must live with the consequences of our past. We don't remember past lives or past incarnations. We will only ever know this life, and yet we are forced to accept punishment for past sins and misdeeds.

Learning to accept is part of the human journey and divine plan. Acceptance gives us the strength to adjust, reset, and redefine who we are and can be, both as individuals and as a global society. Without acceptance, we trap ourselves in thinking injustices can be overcome. Then like hamsters trotting on a large running wheel, thinking we are progressing, we remain captive to an uncompromising fate that has become our life and destiny.

I have accepted my fate. I can't choose a better life. I must complete this life journey with its karmic-imposed sentence to be released and again be given the freedom to choose. As I contemplate this, thoughts of a better life, freed from past accountabilities, starting anew on a clean slate, and being the person I always wanted to fill my mind. This, I know, will never eventuate. I am now aged and old. I no longer have the inclination or strength to seek or enjoy such freedom.

I am contented with what this life has given me. I will not seek more or rebel. I will live peacefully, passively, and justly. I have learned by reliving the many horrors and traumas I had caused, all now etched in my mind. These, I carry as a mental and psychological burden, while knowing this is just punishment for what I had done. I have accepted this. I was responsible for my sins. I can never, therefore, forget what I have done. I only hope I will be able to dispel these thoughts when I die and not carry these to my next life.

What I had done, I now see this global community doing. Soon, I fear, it will be destined to live and suffer a similar fate. What people do as individuals and society, the global community now does. This has now entrapped us all, we all now are travelling on the same path, destined to reach the same destination.

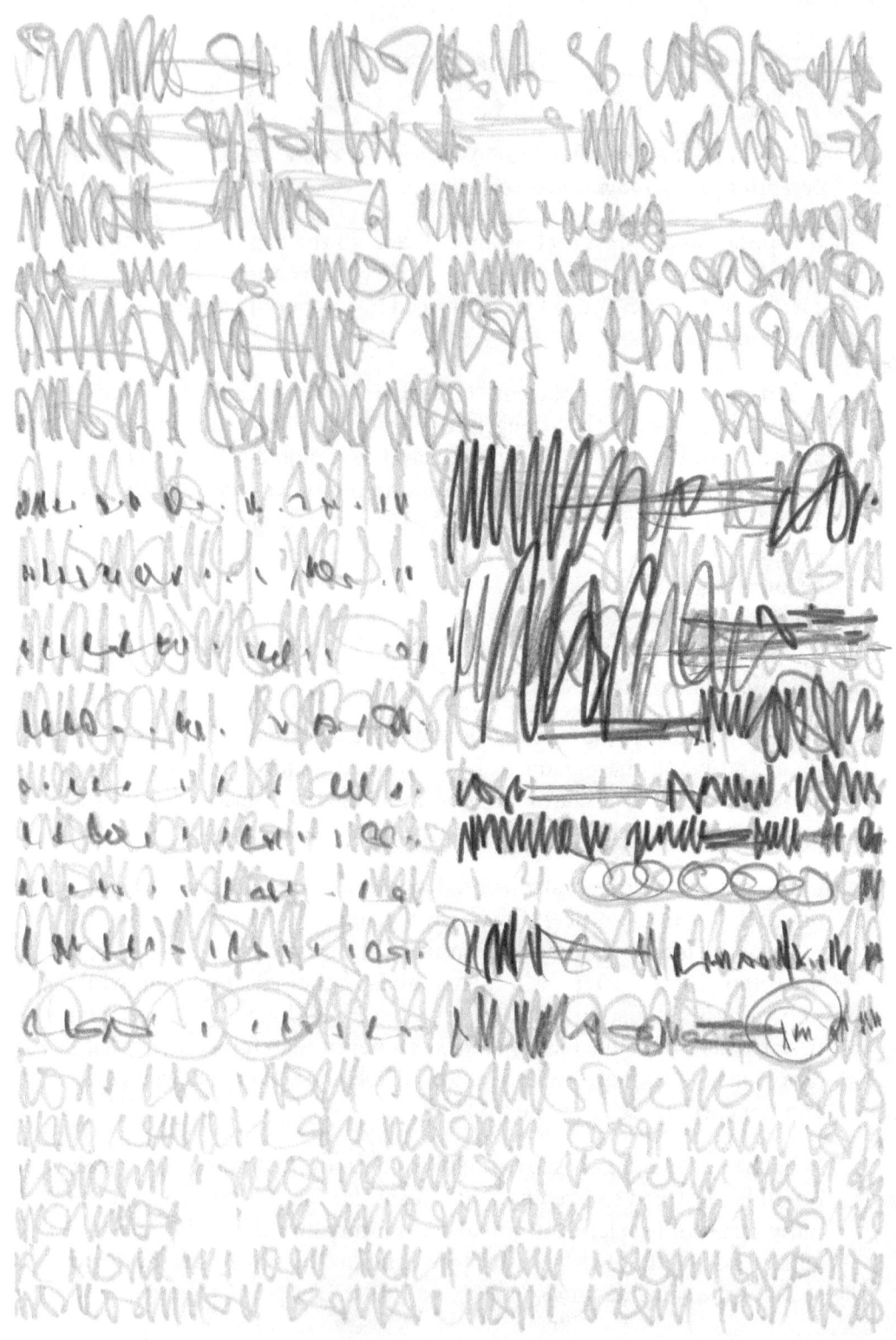

The Personal Dilemma

My life path was preset long ago. I cannot change it. My past, my sins, and the harm I had caused had securely placed me here on this path.

Karma has done this to me. It had manifested to hold me to account and is now forcing me to reconcile the bad I had done. It has done this to stop the unending cycle of trauma I had started.

My deeds had defined me, and my choices had sealed my fate. I had chosen to be bad. I had invited the darkness and evil within. This was my choice, and now this sentenced miserable life is my punishment. I, however, don't recall or know all that I had done. Only karma truly knows all my secrets and all the harm I had caused.

It is karma that monitors and records all interferences and challenges to the universal laws. It then holds those to account who break these laws and cause imbalances. Everything we do, every action and resulting reaction, is monitored. Everything else is then linked and inseparably connected and dependent on what is done and what occurs.

Karma monitors all and intervenes when extremes and imbalances occur. This it does before these escalate to devastate completely. This is why karma had sentenced me, set my destiny, and is now forcing me to face and reconcile my past so one day I can be forgiven.

My soul is still deeply marred with the evil I had long carried. I had followed many false and fake prophets who promised eternal life and salvation. These people had intentionally manipulated me to gain some pleasure or benefit and then left me with a heavy-burdened past that stained me.

I cannot change my past, nor do I have explanations or reasons for what I did. And nor does karma allow me to discuss this with others. When I try, my mind and body freeze into inaction as if cursed by a spell. This dilemma has become part of my journey, which is leading me to redemption. I alone must travel this path until I reach its very end. This is my journey.

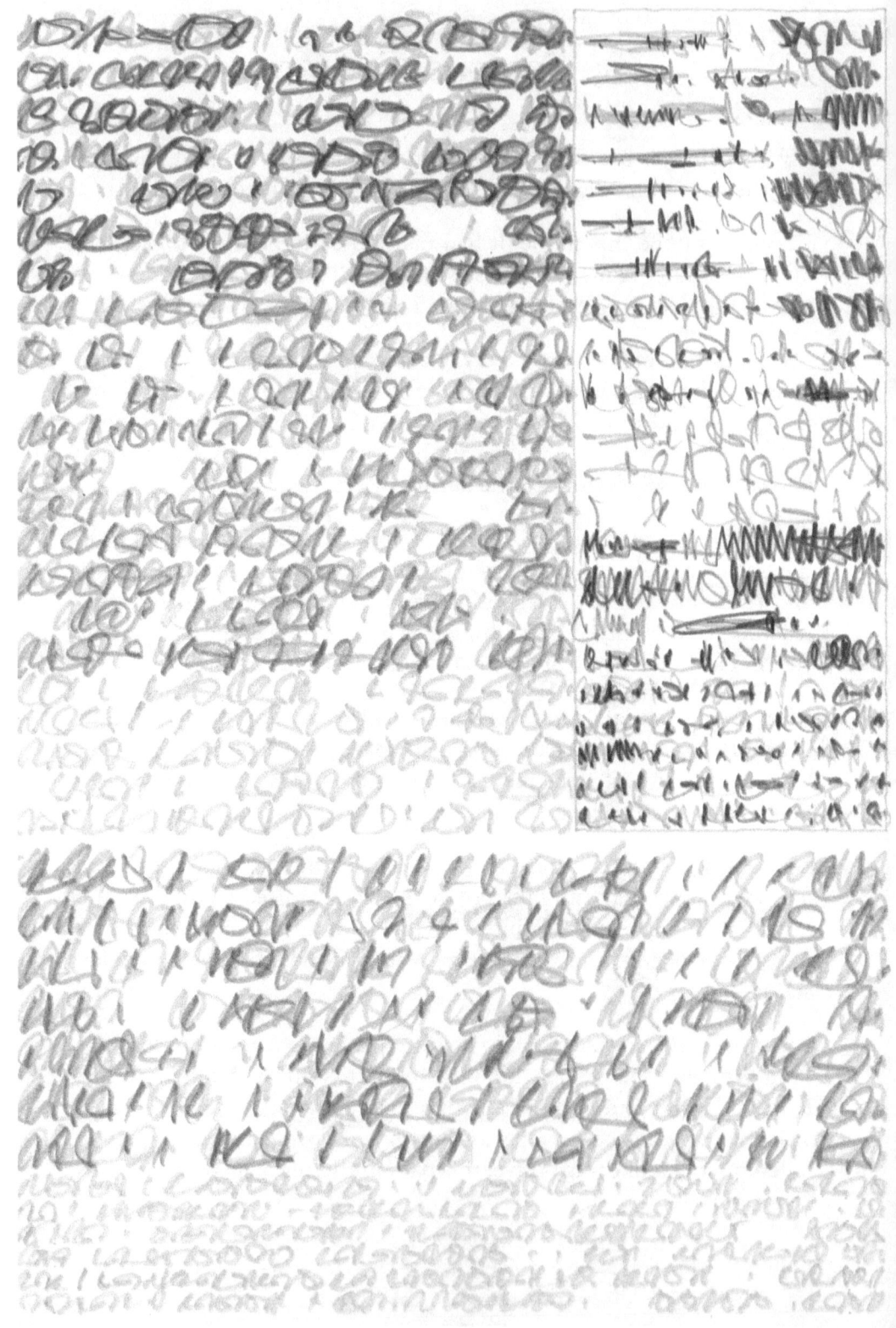

The Social Dilemma

Can you not see the stain spreading into every part of society and our environment?

If you choose to look, you will see many present and irresolvable dilemmas. Each is a problem of our own making that needs fixing.

A global crisis is looming. It has appeared on the distant horizon and is rapidly approaching. This is of our making, as individuals, and as a society. We all have contributed to this. Our actions have caused irreparable global damage that is now harming us and the environment. If we fail to reconcile this and continue to disregard what might occur, the worst will eventuate.

Who we are, what we have, our structured society, how we live, what we do, and our combined choices, decisions, and actions are all aggravating this dilemma. We have prioritised humanity over nature and profits over humanity. Our devised financial systems profit when ecology is consumed and expand as disparity increases between rich and poor.

Despite all our might and technology, we lack wisdom. We readily dismiss the harm we cause as inconsequential. We are free to choose, and yet we have no say as individuals. We all have already forfeited our social power. We allowed financial systems and processes to operate as they will, efficiently consuming, causing harm, without producing any real benefit. What we do and have done has made us globally vulnerable.

There is now climate change. Our world is also in pain with disease and pestilence. We had done this. We manipulated, arranged, created, and installed systems with processes that convert ecosystems into waste. We create crises that disenfranchise many, especially the most vulnerable and those in absolute despair. And we allow this to continue to this day. We do have choices. We don't have to accept the status quo. We can choose to rectify past wrongs. We can protect the environment and provide better lives for the most vulnerable. And if we choose, we can better integrate humanity with nature, society with ecology, and enable an equitable life for all. We, however, lack the will to do so. We prefer to continue as our forebears did, despite knowing this will soon bring judgment day, full of retribution, for all.

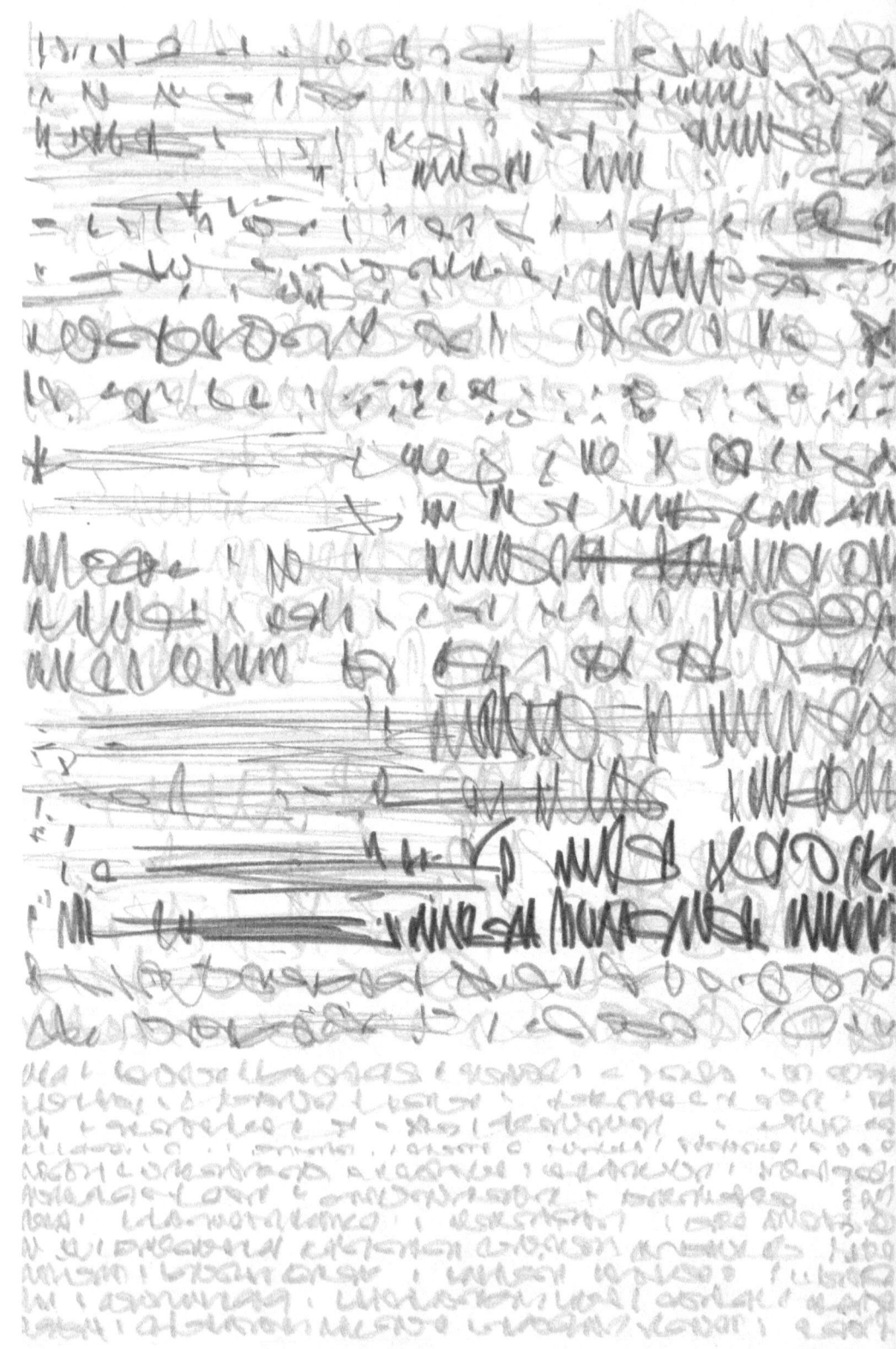

Despised

I was born into a world full of hate.

An invisible yet powerful force has set and determined my fate. At birth, this fate was nailed to my soul, to sentence me and contain the evil I have within. This has since mentally scarred and psychologically traumatised me. I still feel and hear the evil within. It struggles in pain every waking hour, trying to free itself.

As people approach and see me, some sense something is wrong. I see their facial expressions change. They seem to feel the hatred of the evil I have within. This instantly repels them. Others only see what I have become—a worthless vagrant vagabond. These people may be oblivious to what I have within but, nevertheless, avoid me. No one confronts me or asks me who I am or what I have. Everyone chooses to ignore me.

I have become that inconsequential soul that is purposefully dismissed and ignored. Those who do cross my path treat me as if I didn't exist or as a worthless anomaly that sprang into this existence. If I could, I would go back to where I came from.

Maybe it is right for people to be repelled by me. I deserve this.

All my youthful adolescent thoughts of rage, retribution, and unfairness have long vanished. I no longer have or carry such thoughts, nor do I reciprocate when people harm me. My fight is within me, and it requires all my strength to endure and persist.

My past had placed me here, and yet I am still forced to relive it. Memories of all I had done linger in my mind and occupy my thoughts. Each reminds me of who I was and had become—an unforgiven, regressive, and unenlightened persona. This is what evil made me as it still tries to control me. This, I still cannot overcome or dispel.

I sense I have known this evil from the beginning of time. It attached to me, my soul in the deep past when darkness still dominated this world. Since then, it has accompanied me at each incarnation. Only now, in this lifetime, it has finally met its match with karma. Karma has suppressed, contained, and caged this evil. This has now given me the means to wrestle with this evil but not the strength to dispel it from my being. This is my curse.

Karma Revisited

My fate is inescapable. Karma had waited for generations to intervene. It had allowed me to live freely, possibly hoping that I would atone for my sins and redeem myself. I, however, continued to accumulate debt with misdeeds, causing substantial pain, misery, and suffering to others. Nor did I reconcile this. I allowed debt to accrue until it had caused an imbalance that forced karma to act, needing to correct this by forcing me to live with its repercussions.

I still have substantial negative energy that weighs heavily on my mind and soul. When I do good, I feel it dissipate temporarily, however, returning soon after with a vengeance. Karma monitors this, while it ensures I continue to repay my debt. As it waits, it metes out daily punishments that dispel the negative energy I have. This also ensures my pain and misery is constant as I try to reconcile what I have done and settle my karmic account.

We can all incur karmic debt by simply diverting from the just path. Karma tallies this and it will also judge what we had done. All the bad, all the misdeeds that caused evil to manifest or the stain to spread, are tallied and considered.

Karma is that eternal omnipresent force that manifests to fight evil. It resides within the cosmic realm that envelopes this universe. It can reach anywhere and everywhere on this plane. And when an imbalance does occur, it manifests to stop the spread and restore order. Karma is also an enigma that is beyond comprehension or understanding. Rather than acknowledging it, we choose to dismiss what it does as providence, fate, or God's will. Only sentenced souls know the truth.

Without reason, we don't question what it is or what it does. We prefer to surround ourselves with a deafening noise of misinformation that dulls our intellect and reduces our understanding. With this, we also separate ourselves from the truth and reality while allowing others, our leaders, to inform and guide us. We then become complicit as we listen and follow, helping the corrupt spread their stain, damning us all from within.

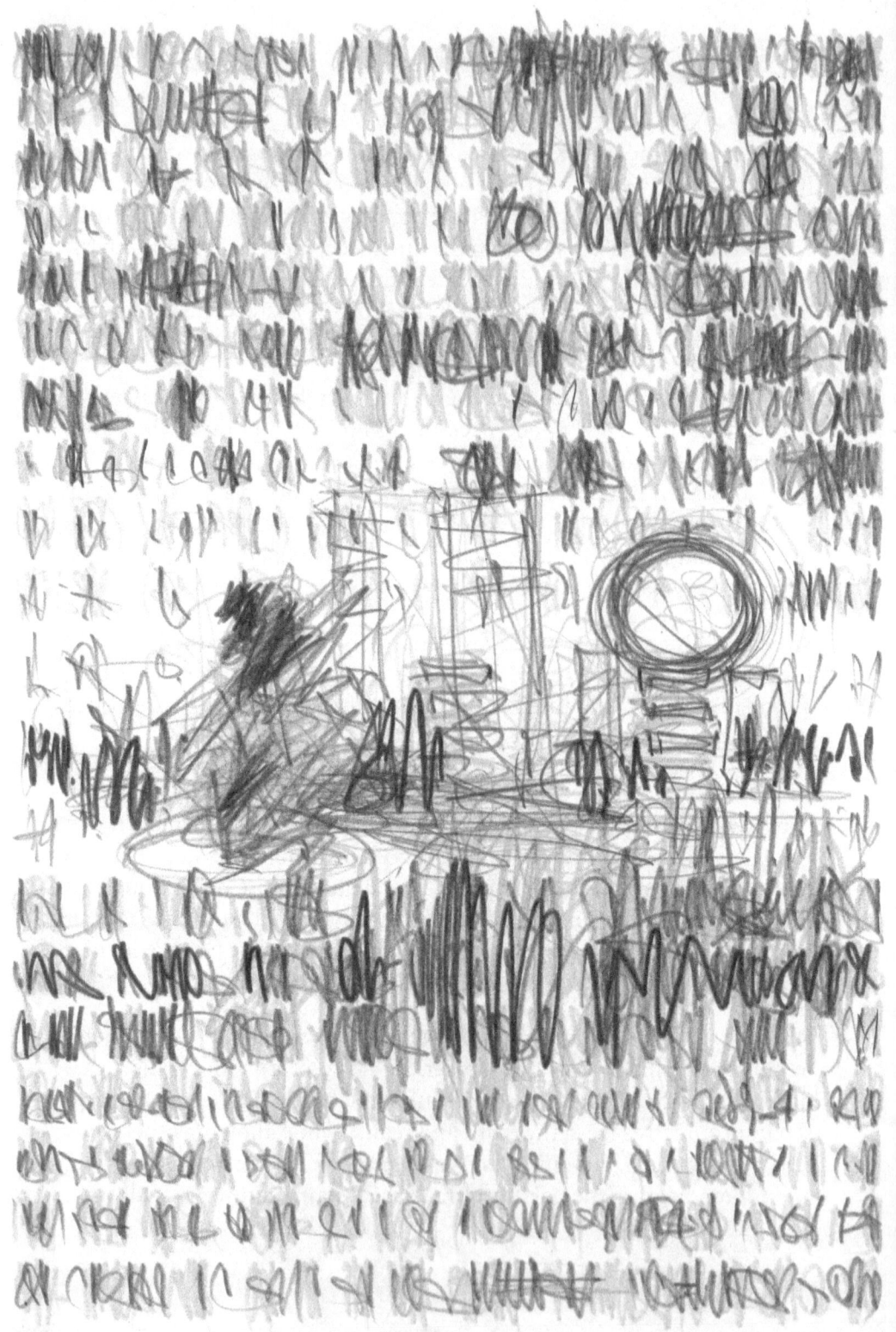

Neurosis and Depression

Is free will and self-determination more important than abiding by universal laws?

Freedom is an illusion. No one is truly free or ever will be. We are all controlled by laws and rules. We break these by doing bad. We then must live with the repercussions and consequences of this wrong.

There is plenty of leeway and leniency with the bad we do. There is also ample opportunity to atone for our sins and reconcile what we had done. But by choosing to be persistently bad and failing to make amends, karma will soon intervene to hold us to account.

Karma remembers all we had done. It knows our past, sees the present, and does not forget. We, however, are unable to recall or remember what we had done during past incarnations. We are all programmed to forget. Our memory corrupts as we age and resets at rebirth.

All we do remember, however, will inadvertently be distorted by time and a failing mind. Equally, our selfish desires, thoughts, and life itself will corrupt our memories. With choice, we conveniently can also reset memories, so as to forget the bad we had done. New thoughts and ideas then seed and germinate to create false memories that support an alternate reality based on our own selfish needs. Despite all this, the truth remains and cannot be replaced or erased.

We, therefore, should not fool ourselves. If we purposefully attempt to alter our truth, we can easily lose ourselves within an alternate reality of our own making. This will then likely corrupt our minds and diminish our worth. Our existence is not fake or illusionary as experienced by Don Quixote de La Mancha. Keeping things real is important and vital as only this enables the truth to be understood as well as who we are, were, and can become.

Questioning the Definitive Truth

Is this real? Is there an absolute truth?

Do you not see or understand what is happening? Don't you know how connected we all have become and what occurs then will similarly affect us all? Or do you prefer to believe our future is assured?

When you see people suffering, do you purposefully try to avoid them? Are you afraid this might reveal an uncaring nature? Is there some past unresolved injustice that makes you see their suffering as just punishment?

Do you not consider yourselves foremost, above all else? Do you not feel righteous despite being wrong? Do you not know how complicit you have become with all the bad that occurs? Do you not care about the consequences of our combined actions?

The information we receive with its many falsehoods and half-truths has separated us from reality. The daily news that is fed to us is purposefully formulated to misguide, suppress, manipulate, and indebt us to a corrupt system.

Do you know what the full and complete truth is?

Half-truths with misinformation are used to control and manipulate society. This occurs to quell our social power, so we don't object or fight for what is right.

Those who do this, know the complete truth of this reality. They claim truth is trivial, inconvenient, and can be dismissed. They say this, as they replace it with a manipulated truth, full of lies and deceit. This they do, proclaiming to maintain world order while profiting from the lies they tell and benefiting the powerful and rich.

As we listen to their lies, we have become what these manipulators had wanted us to become: a subservient, ineffective, depressed, anxious, obsessive, hypochondriac, and a mentally-ill society. And as they continue to manipulate the truth, we, the misinformed, then suffer while the powerful continue with their evil intent.

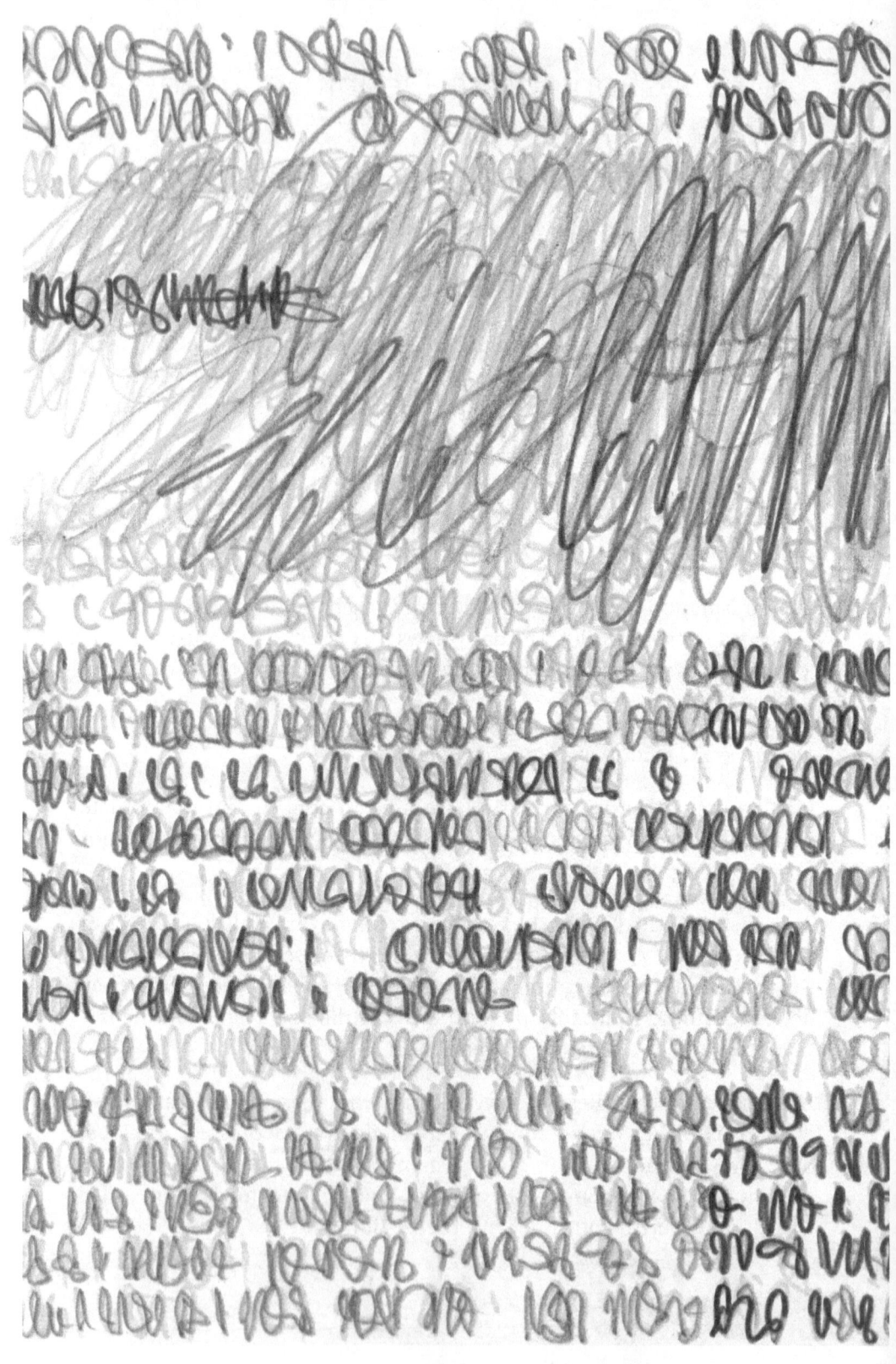

Wishful Thinking

Thank you, God, for the many blessings you bestowed onto me and for giving me the life I have. Only you know best.

Wishful thinking had always led me to trouble and despair. I had always known that I would never be reprieved or my sentence commuted. During this life, I simply had to learn to endure. I had to persist to overcome. This is how I also managed to dull the constant and ongoing pain that I feel each day.

No matter how much I wished, I never could improve my condition. My suffering continues with mental torture that never eases or ceases. Remnant haunting memories of horrid acts replay in my mind each second of each day. Even while drugged, in a self-medicated state, there is no respite. Drugs only heighten my awareness and depression.

The last years were horrible for me. Hope had vanished, along with all opportunities to improve my condition. Life became a miserable trial filled with despair. Karma had used all its might to punish me further and severely. Each day was a struggle that eventually became an ordeal.

As within, so without—the law of correspondence.

In late 2019, evil unleashed its pandemic onto this world to cause misery and death. By the end of 2020, 1.26 million people died. By end of 2021, this had increased to 5.5 million. As this climaxed, there was no immediate help, care, or remedy for the affected. Rather, this pandemic revealed the awful truth, our uncaring nature for life, and the reality of our deep vulnerabilities.

At first, political and spiritual conmen arose to calm and dispel fear, proclaiming there was no real concern. As false news propagated, this fueled many half-truths, spreading with the contagion, causing social upheaval. And when our leaders and industry mobilised, they produced lethal vaccines to contain the virus, which then harmed us all.

This was also the time society forgot its poor, the disenfranchised, and the destitute. There was no reprieve for their misery as they suffered. Fates were sealed, as all means to digress were removed. This, we learned as the pandemic began to subside, as we also finally began to understand how selfish we had all become.

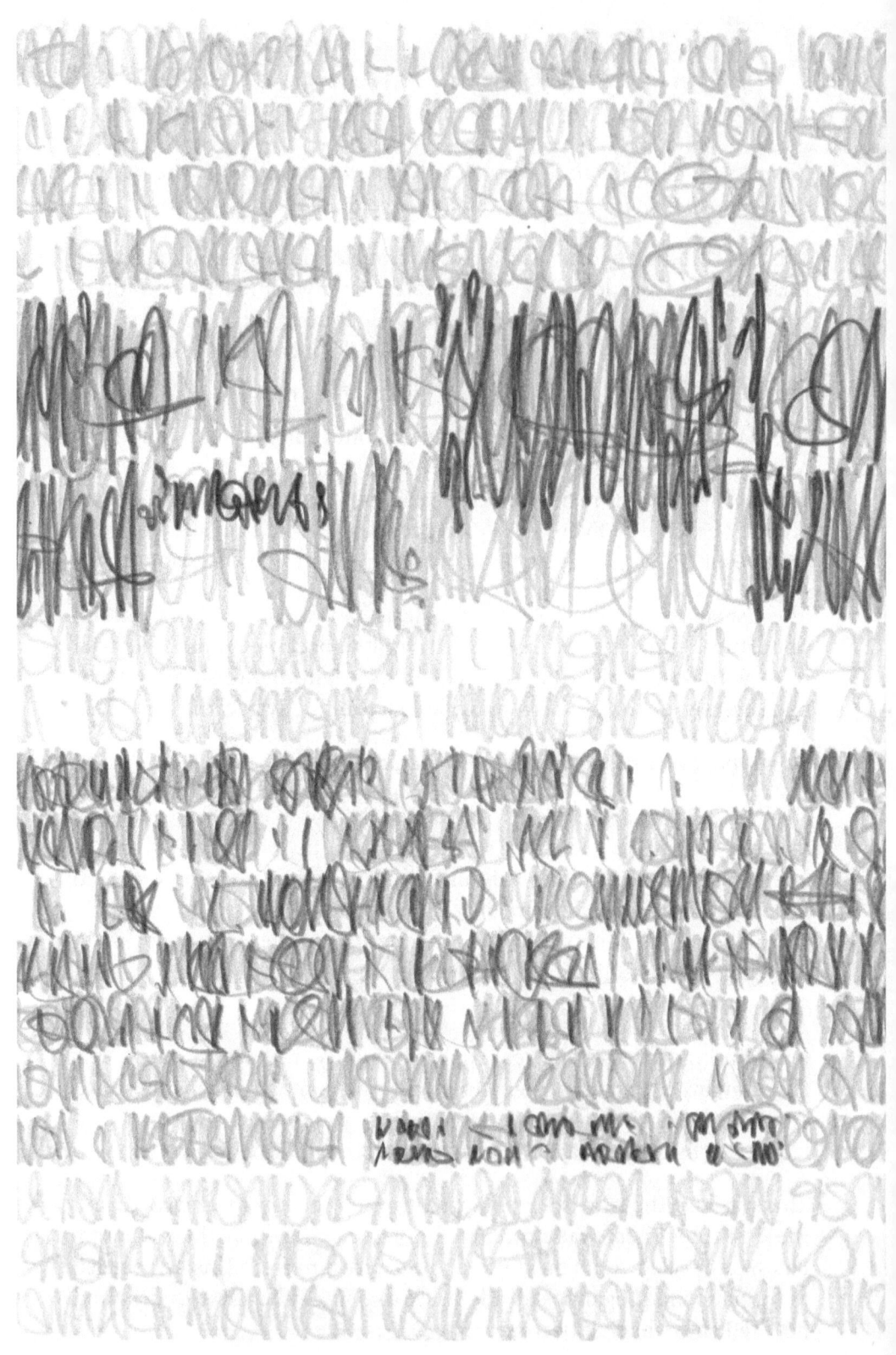

Social Regression

After yet another mass shooting, in another public school, we may think we are living in violent and tumultuous times, more so than any other period in human history. The truth is violence has always been a mainstay of human history. It had made us who we are. It is what we do. It is ingrained in our culture and is how our society has functioned for eternity. It is real, it is here now, and it will continue while we live and exist.

History has recorded many such moments, each detailing how society regressed to devolve with bloodshed. These were the dark times that were spurred by egotistical powerful people promising salvation while delivering death. Their self-interest drove them to create crises that purposefully spiralled society into violent times. Humanity was not a victim but complicit. We had allowed these despots, strongmen, and radicalised savants to lead us and do as they pleased. They changed us, as we fell prey with tribal herding, believing the improbable and the irrational but compelling rhetoric. We readily dismissed and relinquished all that was sacred to participate, including our thoughts, rights, obligations, and responsibilities. With this, our guilt was then deflected to blame the innocent and the disenfranchised. With this, we allowed democracy to disintegrate. We allowed our freedoms to be taken from us. We allowed governing elites to enact draconian laws and apply ruthless controls that infringed on our well-being. Rather than providing security, this heightened our social fear, tilting the delicate balance, taking society to a precipice where any further jolt or irrational act would rip the social fabric apart and irreparably harm us all. When secrecy with misinformation disguises the truth, we simply don't see or understand what is happening. Without this, we are unable to prepare for the change that will be forced on us. This happens because of our complacency and the self-absorbed, selfish grind of this life we all have. The fightback to regain lost freedoms will commence when individual thoughts and actions combine with our social might. Together, we can champion goodness; we can challenge and rectify wrongs, sins, and misdeeds, as these occur. Together, we can ensure no further harm occurs and, thereby, also prevent evil from manifesting here again in our midst.

The Realisation

Here I stand at this crossroads, begging, clothed in rags. No one looks or sees me. People hurry past without glancing or acknowledging my presence or dilemma. I feel an indifference with discontent when people inadvertently brush against me. When someone does speak to me, I only hear some selfish demand, seeking to benefit from what I have and know. This is a place without acceptance, pity, respect, or understanding.

I don't fully understand why I am here or why this has become my home, life, predicament, and reality. Nor do I know what others do here, feel, or think when they see me.

No one here cares to understand what I am going through. No one here will ever appreciate or understand the pain and anguish I feel.

When bystanders see me, they may wonder and speculate, drawing their own conclusion, possibly derived from some past biased personal experience. No one will truly know the pain I feel. True understanding requires owning and living the experience, walking in the victim's shoes, seeing, feeling, and living their reality complete with their anguish and trauma.

I had bottomed. I had allowed myself to regress to some fragile, needy, primitive life form. I had reached that near-Neanderthal regressive state that devolved me with numbness and inaction. I have been here before. This condition, I have to transcend to progress and recover.

This is not the beginning nor the end but midway along my journey. While I stay here, I prolong my journey and misery. This, however, has become an arduous ordeal that pains me, making me suffer while I remain here. I am, however, not ready or prepared to progress. This is how I continue to repeat past mistakes as I again succumb to temptation. I alone have cursed myself.

As I contemplated my dilemma, I then finally begin to understand. I had always known the truth. I had wished this on myself. I had set my fate and chosen this journey. I had damned myself so I could later redeem myself. This is what I always had to do. I also knew in the end, karma would intervene to stop me, punish me, and then save me.

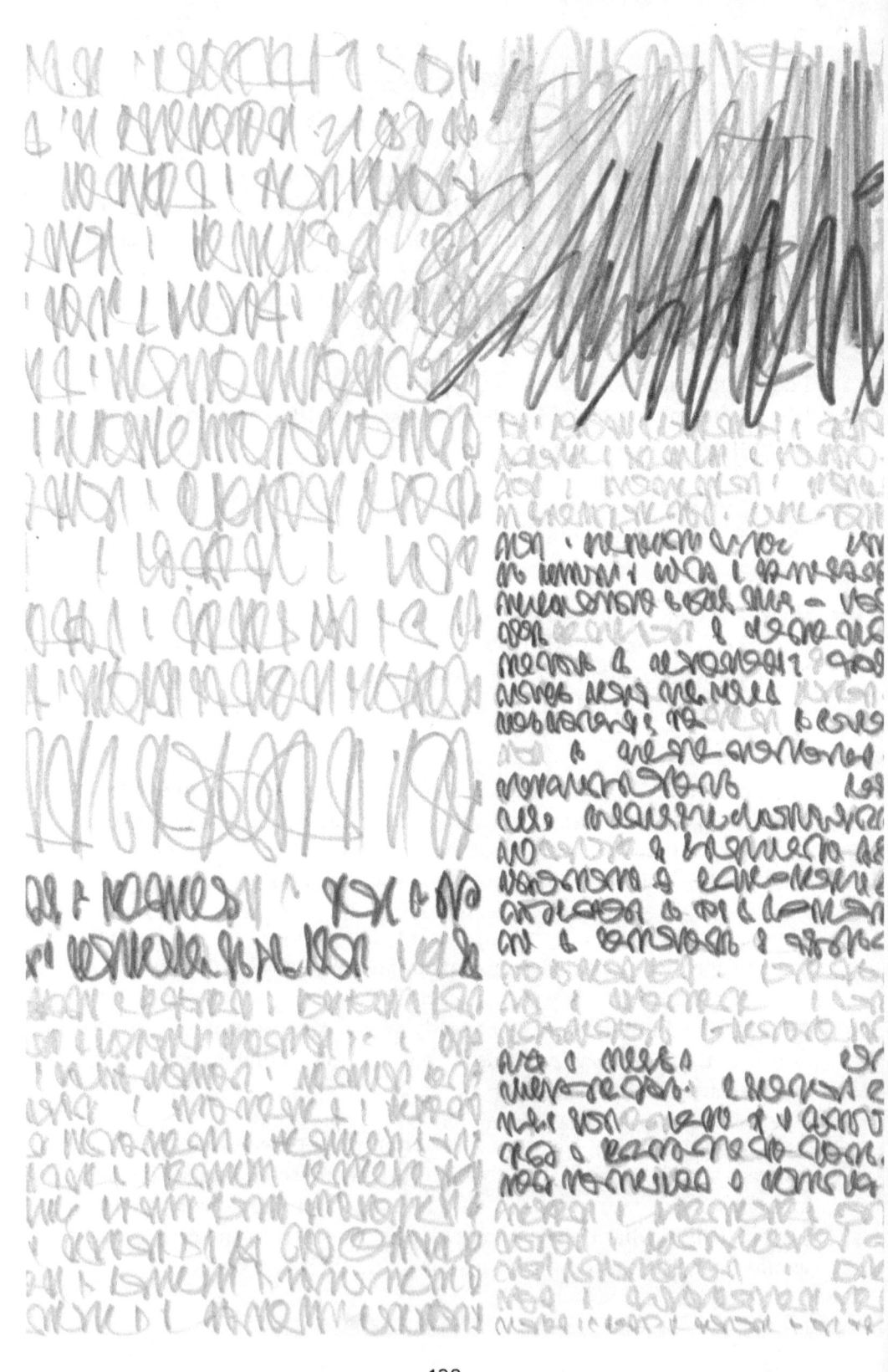

The Misfortune around Me

In determining my fate, karma had weight all my badness against my goodness. This set my fate and sentence. This is why I am placed here. Here, I must redeem myself. I must atone for my sins and reconcile all the bad I had done. And I know this sentence and my miserable life is just punishment for this, what I had done.

What affects me most is the evil entity I still have and carry within. This, I am unable to dispel. The evil within uses all its means to ensure misery and misfortune follow me wherever I go. This it does by affecting and traumatising everyone who comes close and associates with me. I cannot stop or prevent this. I had not wished this on others, and nor do I want to be the source of their misfortune. All I want is to be normal and lead a simple life.

During my youth, I can now recall how I amused myself, contemplating the chaos and harm I could cause and how I would see others suffer. Now older, I am also wiser. This thought now traumatised me. I now feel the misfortune and misery unfolding around me. To stop this, I purposefully avoid contact with others, hoping this simple act will stop evil from harming them.

I have seen both my brothers die. My mother fled from the household and family because of me. I saw my father also change. He lost hope when he realised the dilemma of this situation. He then left, became destitute, and soon died. When I could no longer tolerate the misery of this, I also left. I chose isolation so I could contain the evil within me.

Eventually, I lost contact with everyone I knew, all my kin, my friends, and my family. Now alone, I simply keep moving, travelling, purposefully to keep distance and separate myself from friends and acquaintances.

This has become a lonesome journey. I am now without friends or family and have no reason to settle or seek comfort. I simply keep moving, wandering aimlessly, trying not to attach to places, people, or anything. As I wish to dispel the cursed evil I have within, I also wish I could end my miserable existence.

The Forgotten

As I walk, a series of memories flood my mind and fill my thoughts. These are the residual memories of my past lives. Each lost, long-forgotten damned memory awakens some victim who then seeks vengeance and restitution. Each had suffered by me, by my hand and my misdeeds. Each also asks me why. I, however, don't remember and can't answer. As these memories linger, I feel pushed, prodded, and forced to dwell deeper into my past.

Am I losing my mind? Is this real? Have I met these souls in the past? Is this mental anxiety that is consuming me? Or are these implanted thoughts from some alternate reality? Or has my deep past simply caught up with me, which I am now forced to remember?

I sense I was not meant to forget these memories. The people I had harmed are now trapped within my mind, occupying my every thought. Each wants me to acknowledge them and remember what I had done. What I recall, however, is a fractured past that I am not yet able to piece together. I can only glimpse at what might have occurred. But as I digress, doubt fills my mind, and I begin to distrust these recollections, questioning whether this is real.

How is it possible to recall people and places I had not known existed? Why can't I dispel these memories and thoughts from my mind? Why is this happening now, at this time? Is this part of my sentence?

These are persistent memories that keep percolating through my mind. As each thought replays, I see how I had wronged people. I try relentlessly to stop these thoughts, forcing myself to believe these memories are someone else's and not me, nor my history. I keep assuring myself that I did no wrong and don't have to acknowledge or reconcile this, only to realise this is exactly what I must do to end this. I must help these hurt and tortured souls so they can leave the nightmarish forsaken realm that they occupy in my mind.

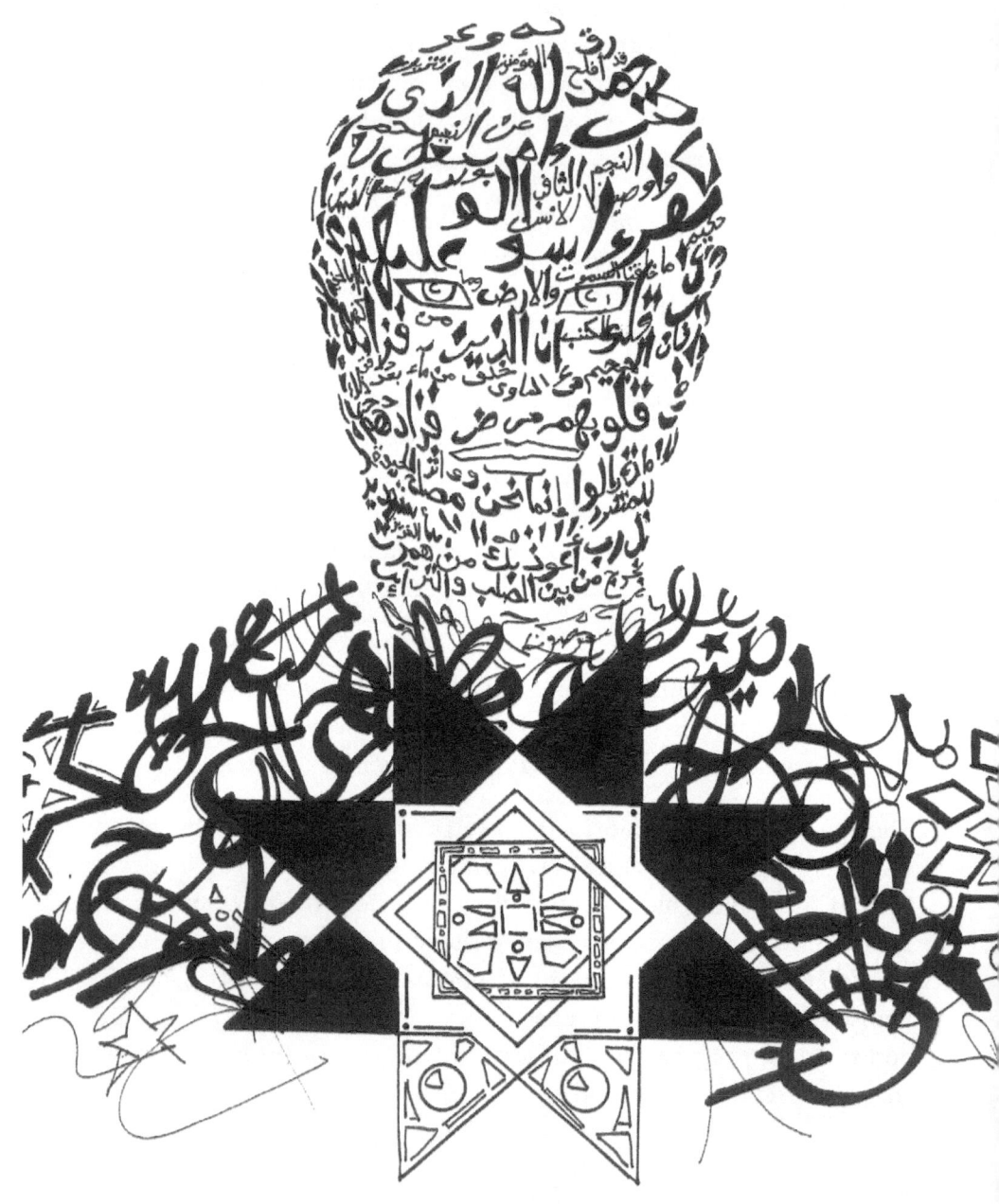

La Mancha

Self-Expression

Do you not see the evil within me?

My face, body, and skin offend people. I feel despised. People look at me in disgust, possibly thinking I am evil incarnate. I notice people purposefully avoiding me, moving away, fearing they will similarly be tainted. This, what I notice, does not affect me; only my own truth does. It haunts me. It fills my mind and appears on my skin. At times it is visible to all. Rather than confront this, I leave, hide, and seek solace and peace by isolating myself.

How can I reconcile my anguished, frightening appearance? Why am I despised? Why can't I redeem myself?

I have tried to conceal my truth by expressing pain. I allow others to mark and ink my body. I now carry many superficial scars, all also covered with tattoos. Each obscures part of me. Each also portrays part of my miserable existence. They have become me, part of my being. This is all others now see. This is me.

My God-given appearance had always disturbed me. I did not recognise who I was or saw in my reflection. The person who looked back at me in the mirror was not me. All I saw was anguish.

To cope mentally and remain sane, I needed to shield my inner self from society. I needed some barrier between me, my soul, and the outside world. I needed to feel comfortable with who I was and what I saw. I needed some type of transformation to help me endure this life. It was then that I found ink. I have since covered my whole body with ink, purposefully tattooing and scarring my body until I felt comfortable. Ink transformed me. It erased my former self and freed me. I now feel impregnable and can finally move freely and do as I want. Ink has also given me art. As I move my body, I see new patterns form, each reflecting my circumstances and mood.

My inked networked lines and images have since gained their own presence. They have become more than my shield, my body armor, they now allow me to hide in plain sight. This is who I have become and am. Each tattoo and scriptured line is now part of me. Each reflects who I am and reveals my truth.

Depression and Anxiety

The oldest and strongest emotion is fear, and the strongest fear is the fear of the unknown.

From my vantage point, I can see how our leaders, those who profess to represent us, those we have entrusted; the government officials, corrupt themselves. They act freely, carelessly wielding the power they acquired from us. I see how they benefit as they manipulate us, proclaiming to be our saviours, while causing mayhem and destruction, as they also lead our society to a precipice.

The hopelessness I feel has become my predicament. It has made me anxious. Despair engulfs me as I am led to a point of no return and to a time when everything will end. I follow those who lead me. I have accepted their leadership. I do what they ask of me, even succumbing to the temptation of greed, envy, and pride, all to appease them.

I, like many, follow these people, striving to gain some status and station in life. As we follow, we consume needlessly and do unconscionable things that wontedly destroys the remaining goodness that exists. This, what we do, we know is unsustainable, and yet we continue.

There is no will to change or improve. We banish, disenfranchise, and cast out those who rebel or resist. There is no social justice. We simply admire the powerful. We see them as our saviours while we forsake all our remaining goodness. Social greed drives us to participate. We think we are doing good, only to find ourselves corrupted and implicated as we take this world to its end.

Those who realise the truth also know what is at stake. They know there can be no immediate change as dissention is quickly quashed. Controlled, we fear the thinly-veiled threats of extreme violence might eventuate. We know the power our leaders wield will quickly overwhelm and silence us. Unable to respond or act, we procrastinate, damning ourselves further. We cower as fear paralyses, thinking we too might be held responsible for what occurs, only to realise our inaction has caused this. We had all misjudged this, our situation. The state had tricked us to believe we would be kept safe while it made us dependent and vulnerable. This social dilemma we must set straight and reconcile.

Temperance

I still have to find my place in this world. This, I seek while yearning to know the complete truth. I have long relied on my beliefs, thinking this was where I would find answers. This, however, has always clouded my mind and filled my thoughts with raw emotions and feelings that stymied my progress. To start again, I must first clear my mind, dispel such thoughts, and transcend through my past to find the truth. This, I know, will set me free.

As I endure and persist with what is, I allow my mind to retrace where I had been. I methodically begin questioning all I had done and known, deciphering what I did right and wrong. As I regress, I find no goodness in my past. I did not produce or give. I only took and consumed.

As I contemplated this, I find I no longer need to indulge or consume. I am not a starving animal. I do not need to gulp food quickly down for fear of losing it to others. Nor do I need to eat or drink to live. This is not living. As I think this, I find I cannot remember why I had done this or why I allowed this to become the essence of life. I want to again associate with the living. To do so, I need to feel hunger pains and feel the struggle to survive. I needed this understanding so I could continue with my life.

Deep in thought, I begin to comprehend how related the personal, social, and spiritual matters are. To overcome evil, we must contribute with goodness and help stop the mass-indulgence that is sickening society. I can help by giving and reducing my impact on this world. With sufficient charity, I can help reduce the disparity that affects so many. Everyone and everything deserve a fair share and the right to live. With what little I do, I hope to encourage others to participate.

With this, I can finally forgive myself for the bad I had done. I now understand how each small gesture matters; each contribution with goodness has some positive effect. Each also encourages others to act appropriately, collaborate, and helps direct the ongoing change that is occurring. We all can influence what is to occur and what can transpire. Every small gesture helps.

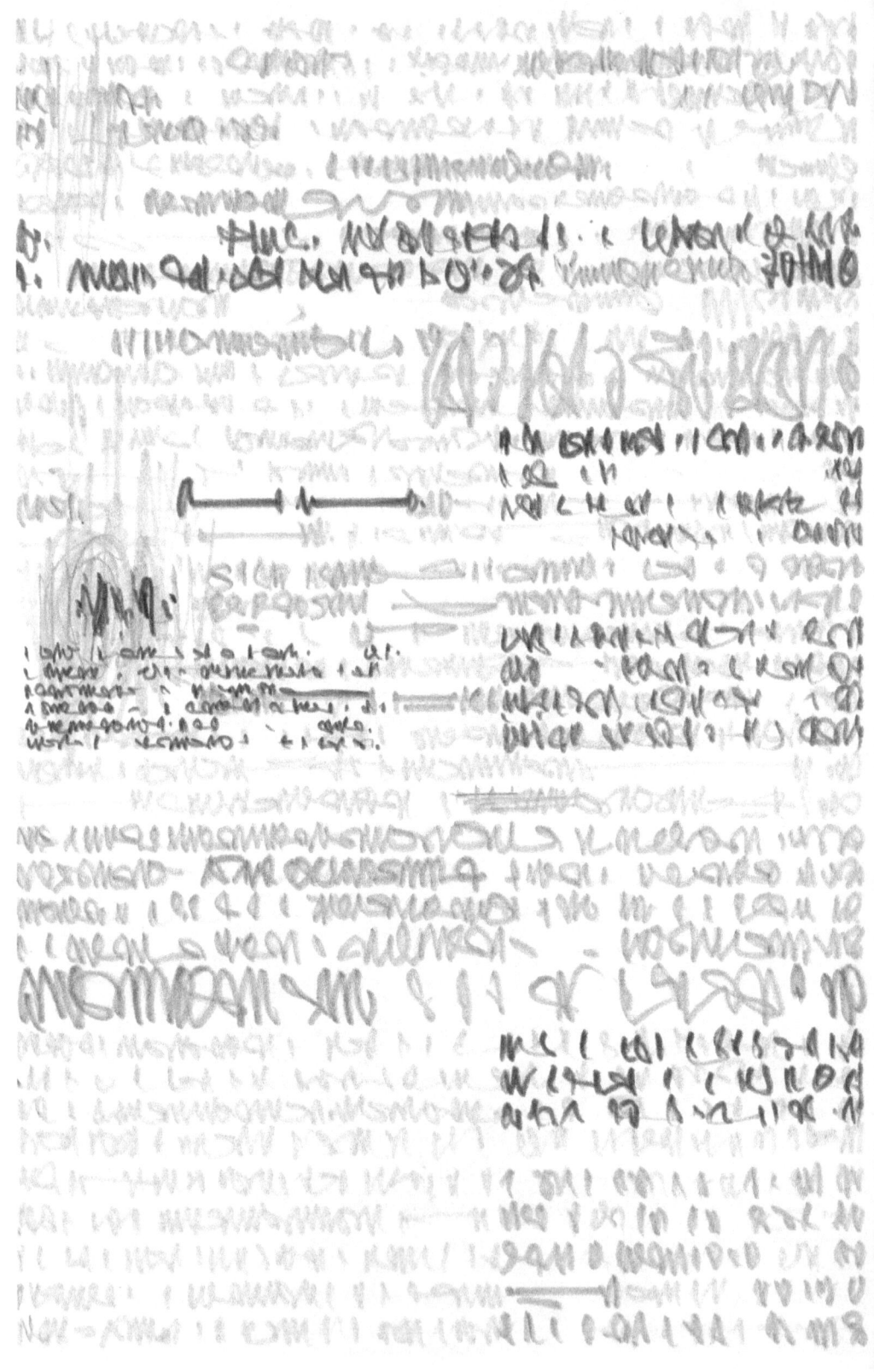

Charity and Generosity

Joy is in giving while not expecting anything in return.

We are the only species on earth that takes without giving back. We take to consume and possess. This, our innate, selfish nature, is greedy for materialism. We are all corrupted, unable to unreservedly give. A lustful gluttonous consumption desire always tempts us to consume more than we need. As we succumb to this, we then also dismiss the sacredness and true value of life. Our continued taking has created a huge imbalance that will soon need to be reconciled.

Consumption is not our god nor our saviour. It is our vice. This, we must learn to control, temper, rein in, and restrain, so as not to damn us completely. This we must replace with charity, compassion, and generosity to others.

Gluttonous temptation had always affected me, physically and mentally. I am enslaved by an irresistible desire to consume. It placed me here, where I now am. My mind and body are corrupt, both succumb easily to tempting thoughts, causing me to falter. I like others, have hunted, harvested, harmed, and taken life to the brink of extinction. This, I now cannot reconcile. All I can do is regret.

I am desperate to transcend my past with my tainted self. I want to break all bonds with the past as I yearn to establish a sustainable balance with life. I have to stop succumbing to corrupting influences with their indulgent strivings. I have to control my envy, my pride, and the senseless anger that I unleash on this world. I need to retire my sense of entitlement and curtail my lust for more. I need to start giving and sharing all I have.

This is what we all must do. We must all transcend our past. Everyone must make this journey together. We cannot wait for some enlightened, righteous soul, elder, or leader to come to guide us. This will never occur. This is a journey we must all choose to make by ourselves and together as a global community.

Patience

Patience and forgiveness are required to endure hardship and attain peace.

This is not me. I am impatient. I have urges I cannot control. The most prevalent is my enraged anger with self-entitled selfish thoughts. I have always succumbed to the vice of wrath as I am a hateful, misanthropic, vengeful person.

I sense everyone has and must learn to control their anger. There exists a deep-seated hatred within us all. It lies mostly dormant within us but brewing inside. Our ancestors gave us this, remnants of centuries-old struggles, feuds, conflicts, and wars. This is an inheritance we cannot fully understand and many cannot control.

Anger is a mainstay of society. It emerges without reason or provocation, possibly triggered by unresolved emotions, yet arising to unleash its terror on all. We are all guilty of unleashing anger onto others, even nations, which allow, without reason, conflict to escalate into war.

We are all partly enslaved and controlled by this vice. Its perpetual nature with spiteful, hateful desires has damned many, including me. I am guilty. I have purposefully hurt and harmed others. I am ashamed this has become me. I cannot control this. Unfounded vengeful thoughts still fill my mind. I cannot erase these. Nor can I calm my inner being or focus on goodness, compassion, or tolerance as this does not exist within me. My past had corrupted me; it had stained my soul and taken all the hope I had so I will never know or attain lasting peace.

Torment still rages within me. The only relief I find is self-harm, which distracts me temporarily so I forget the vengeful pain that consumes me. I cut and scar my body, wishing others would similarly suffer and know my pain. But when I see the pain of others, I selfishly dismiss the hurt as superficial and unwarranted. My thoughts are not of comfort or support, but rather of vengeful retribution for them having shown such weakness. This also stirs the evil I have within, coercing me to escalate the pain by harming those around me. I know there will be retribution and payback for what I had done and still do. But this is who I am, this is how I live my life, and this is how I survive.

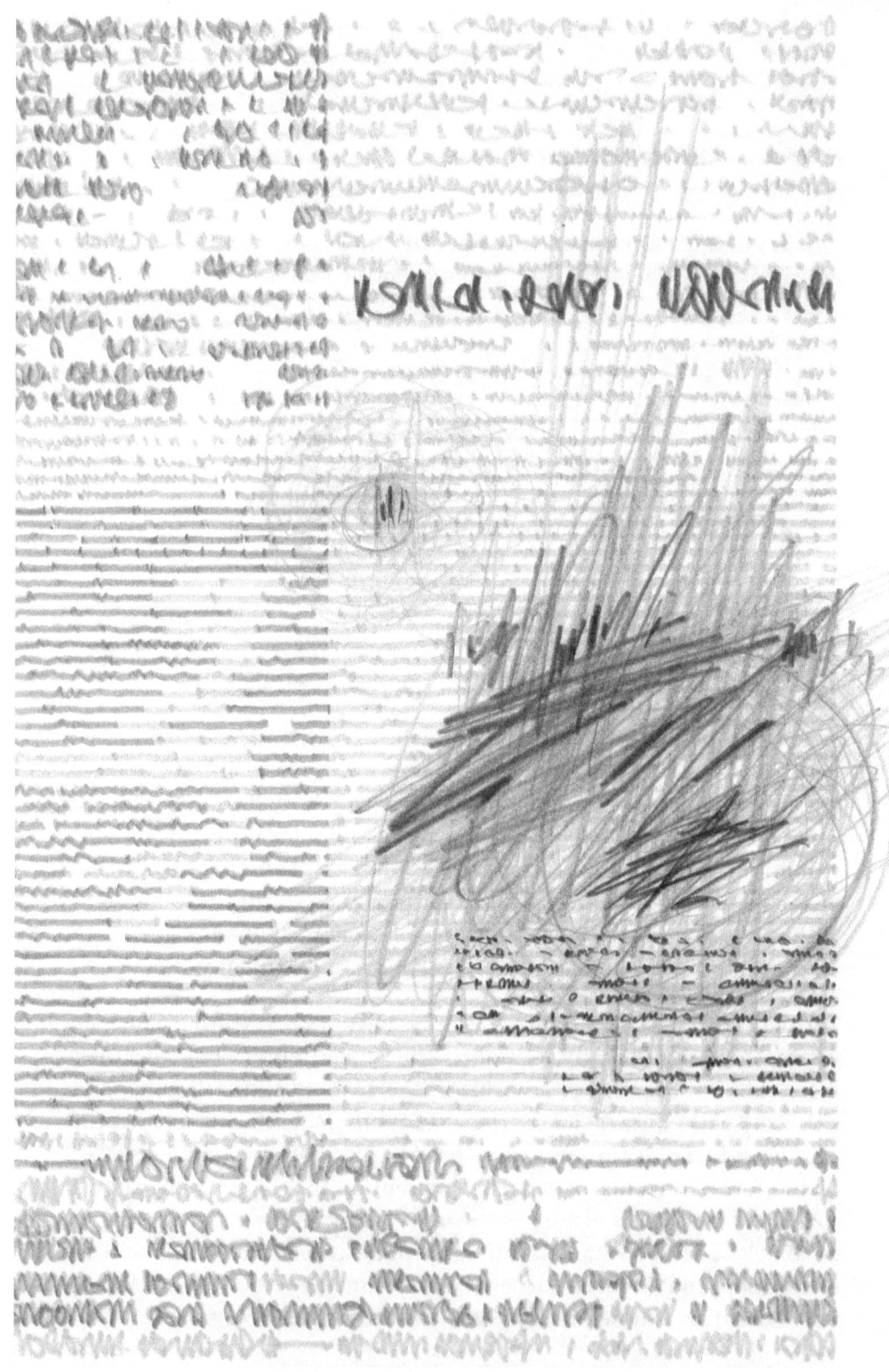

Redemption

We all carry the shame of participating in some past unjust act and evil misdeed.

We all struggle to retain the innocence we were born with. Equally, it is hard to remain on the just and righteous path. Life is an arduous journey, filled with temptation and desires to sin. And as we live life, we must resist temptation and repent, atone and reconcile all our evil thoughts and deeds. We must also readily accept past accusations, together with all retributions to recompense. This we must do with forgiveness, charity, temperance, and chastity. We must also be generous to ourselves and others. This is how we can heal ourselves, become better people, and live a just life.

Living a just or pious life was, however, not for me nor my plan. I had always succumbed to desire and faltered with temptation. Evil always swayed me to stray off the just path. I was always resentful, angry, and spiteful, not wishing to repent or return to the light. I simply did not wish to be confronted with goodness. For me, this was an insurmountable mental journey and quest that I could not make. I would not reconsider or change this thought. This was who I was and why I was sentenced.

I have had ample opportunity to change but could not. For me, change is hard, but a journey I must now make. I need to change to reach redemption. I, however, am still ill-prepared for what I need to do and endure. This, I must do while I serve my sentence which is both demanding and painful. It taxes me heavily. To continue and persist, I must dispel thoughts of failure and reassure myself with affirmations that I am on the right path and I am doing what is right.

As I rest and regain composure, I tap into my inner strength so I can continue and progress. I begin by simply following the light. Suddenly, all the evil thoughts that filled my mind, all the senseless violence, abuse with vengeful anger, selfish, self-serving, and immature desires vanish. With this, I sense a transference occurring. All the previous impediments that once held me back, shackled me to the past, open to release and free me, placing me on a path to redemption.

Remembering Don Quixote

I remembered the story of Don Quixote de La Mancha. I found this tale fanciful, interesting, and intriguing. It was so close to what I was experiencing.

Don Quixote was an ingenious yet insane man who decided to serve his nation by becoming a chivalrous knight-errant. This he did by living in an alternate reality. Don Quixote had managed to transfer his mind to a far-nobler time, to when and where he wanted to be. With this, he escaped reality. Soon, however, the present caught up with him, halted his journey, and shackled him to a live a miserable and accountable life.

Could I be as insane and delusional as Don Quixote? Had I purposefully separated myself from my reality? Do I live an illusionary existence of my own making? Had I inadvertently dismissed the truth and allowed my mind to create this alternate reality? Or did I not know who I was or what I was doing?

The lands where Don Quixote lived were previously stained by the many horrors of war. It had taken centuries to reconcile and cleanse what had occurred there. Peace and calmness now prevailed. There were no longer restraining or controlling forces that dictated or influenced events on these lands. This was all in Don Quixote's mind.

Don Quixote was sick. The disease that had affected his mind opened a portal into the past, to when war was raging and evil was consuming these lands. As his mind wandered, it took him to where he wanted, to where people were suffering through centuries of conflict. He went there to fight evil and help clear the stain from the lands. This became his alternate reality. He wanted to save the world from the evil he saw and felt.

Punishment of Sins

Temporal and eternal punishments are issued when karma comes to redeem and reconcile past misdeeds and sins. Evil is then stopped as stained souls are sentenced and forced to reconcile the bad they had done. Temporal sentences can take multiple lifetimes to complete. Each punishment is full of pain, misery, and suffering served either here on earth or in purgatory. The damned, however, receive an eternal punishment, sentenced, never to return from hell.

Guidance on how life should be lived on earth is in religious doctrine and achieved by applied wisdom and abiding by universal laws. At times, however, this is wrongly manipulated by authorities, purposefully done to misguide us.

During the Middle Ages, the church expanded its authority by giving itself the divine authority to cleanse sinners and remove divine punishment. The church decreed that it could remove all past sins and guilt, and provide forgiveness, restoring a person to a penitent state of grace. With this, it began selling forgiveness by way of a sacrament of reconciliation and indulgences.

It is, however, only God that has the power to grant mercy and forgiveness. And He does so only to those who repent. As it is only by repenting and not by buying forgiveness that sins can truly be forgiven and karmic punishment voided.

God's forgiveness requires the atonement of sins and just punishment for misdeeds. While clemency may be granted, remorse must first be shown, and sins must be atoned with misdeeds reconciled, along with all the bad that was done. If sinners fail to do this and continue to sin, then one-day karma will intervene and hold them to account. The punishment then these sinners receive will likely be life-consuming sentences that they will need to serve until they reconcile all the bad they had done.

Penance and Atonement

Why I, Lord? What have I done to deserve this life?

I don't deserve this. I know I had done wrong, but that was my past; this is now. I have placed my life in your hands, Lord. I accept all the punishment and misery that you will give me. I will continue to repent and atone for my sins until I am forgiven and accepted back to your flock.

Why am I still being punished?

Lord, help me find my way back to you. Help me quell my selfish and foolish pride, and help me heal my corrupted stained soul. Please forgive me. Please help me, Lord.

As I sit and contemplate my dilemma, my mind seems to be guided by an unseen force that directs my thoughts to focus on attaining redemption and forgiveness.

Is this your response, Lord?

I need help and encouragement to continue along the path that has been set for me. I have made promises. I must continue as I simply cannot change course now. There is no alternative but for me to continue, persevere, seeking redemption. As I progress, I try to reconcile all my lesser sins. This I do by changing my behaviour. Soon I find I no longer think the same. A growing righteousness has enveloped my mind, giving me the strength to dispel the thoughts that previously tempted me with desire. This enables me to replace lust with chastity, gluttony with temperance, and greed with charity.

I find temptation no longer taunts me with its evil thoughts. I also feel my nature change. Previously-suppressed hidden and masked feelings and emotions now flood my mind and mentally overwhelm me. Each reminds me of some previous impediment that held me back. As these subside, I gain a newfound clarity with understanding of what was, is, and could be. I feel this begins to heal me from within, physically, emotionally, and spiritually, and gives me new strength and drive to persevere with this fight. I however still have to overcome the evil that still exists within. Despite this being a small change, this has irrevocably changed my life for me. It has also taxed me heavily to reach here, it has consumed most of my inner strength and yet also gives me the relief that I had long sought.

The Indulgence

At the right price, forgiveness can be bought for past and future sins.

It is said only a baptised Catholic who is in communion with the church and does not dissent from the church's teaching can truly be absolved from sin. This, however, comes at a price by the purchase of an indulgence from the church.

The church had professed it could forgive and absolve all past, present, and future sins. It also professed it could absolve deceased loved ones from further punishment. This Roman Catholic indulgence, with its pardons and remittance to absolve future punishment, was sold to benefit the church. From this, the church gained unimaginable wealth and power that then began to corrupt it from within.

The initial sale of indulgences by the Roman Catholic Church began in the late 13th century and lasted until 1567. The Eastern Orthodox Church, however, continued with the sale of absolution certificates until the beginning of the 20th century. All the wealth the church amassed, it then squandered, funding extravagant lifestyles for its priests.

This indulgence-absolution-gate highlighted how greed and wealth can corrupt even the most pious. By professing to have the hand of God, the church allowed its priests to issue indulgences without divine authority. This then stained all the holy, pious, and righteous priests who abused their authority by spreading false hope. As sellers of forgiveness, they were corrupted with greed, while the buyers, who paid for forgiveness were corrupted with false hope and pride.

The sinful sale of forgiveness irreparably harmed and damaged the church as an institution. Before this could be reconciled, it sparked the ecclesiastic revolt that led to the 16th-century Protestant Reformation. As this occurred, it was the believers and the faithful who had pulled religion back from the abyss of corruption, postponing any further retribution.

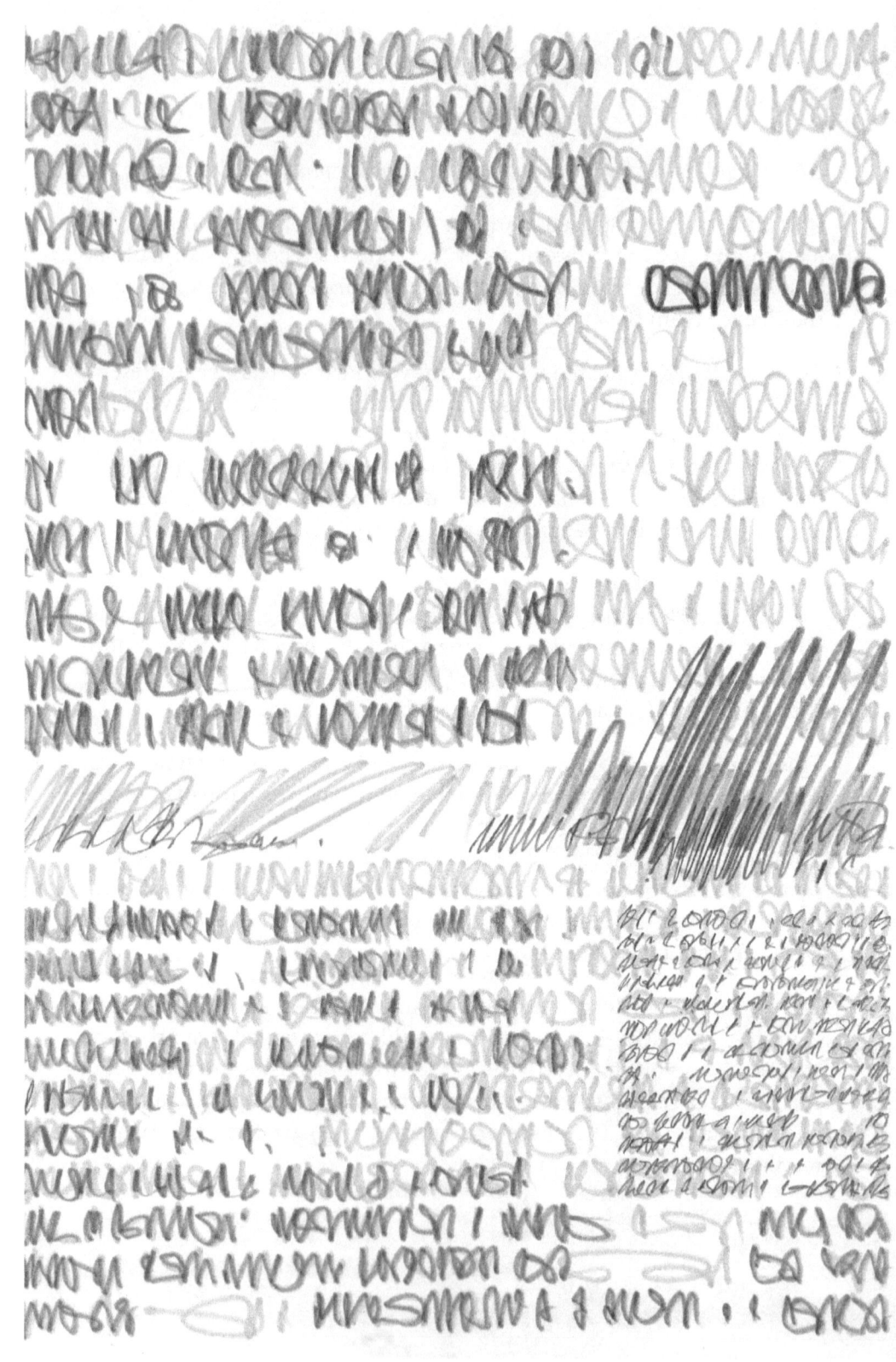
162

The Family

I can no longer keep wandering alone aimlessly. I need rest and company. I had never thought beyond a day or looked beyond my visible horizon. I had remained close to the present, as only this brought stability and gave me meaning with assurance in life. I could not plan or think about the future as only karma determined this for me. I had understood life by living in the present, day-to-day. Each day I knew what I had to do. Then one day everything changed. A thought entered my mind that expanded and evolved my thinking. I saw my visible horizon expand exponentially and move to infinity. I gained foresight. I began to understand there was more to daily existence. This, though, soon separated me from all I previously knew. I felt isolated. I sensed the futility of everything. I began to seek company and find a place to settle. I no longer could accept who I was or how I was living life. I had lost my purpose and direction in life. And while aimlessly searching, I stumbled and found what I needed. This was unexpected and an extraordinary occurrence. I had met a group of like-minded individuals who welcomed me without prejudice. Each seemed to genuinely care for me and my well-being. Each helped me rediscover myself and understand who I was and had become. I had formed a close relationship with each of this household, all unrelated individuals and yet with a common interest. They supported me. They helped me resolve issues and contain my suffering. I was no longer alone. I realised there were many people like me, all carrying some emotional scar from some previous traumatic event. We were all on the same path. We all seek salvation and want to be redeemed. Finally, here, I was at ease with myself, with who I was, and who I had become. Together, here, I also feel stronger. The support I receive nourishes me mentally, physically, and spiritually. I can now see and feel the importance of family and community. There is power within a collective. We all gain something from living together within this group. Each person has some influence that adds to life and expands the possible. I, however, soon found myself at odds with this group. The evil I still have inside was conflicted with the goodness I felt. This affected me and my new friends. I soon felt uncomfortable and removed. I was still a sentenced stained soul burdened by many misdeeds. I then decided to leave before my vulnerabilities and evil would weaken this group.

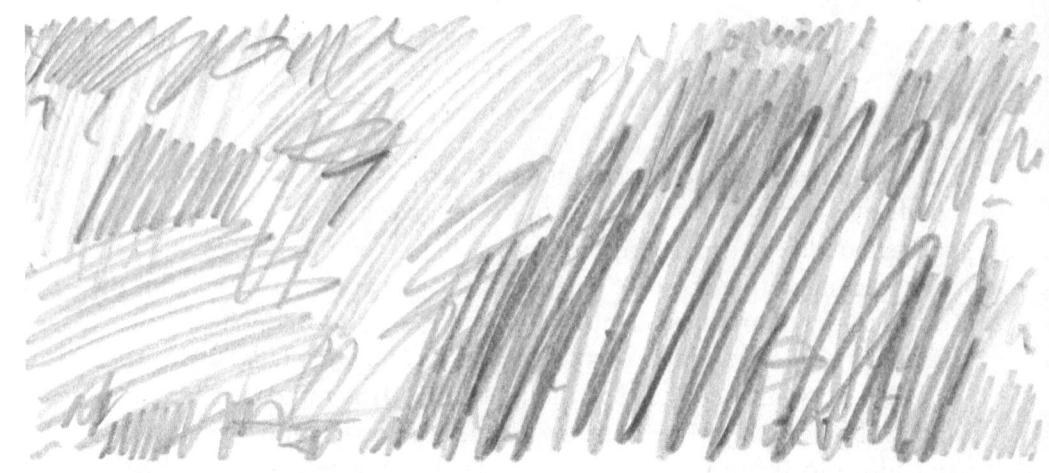

Love Gained and Lost

We are born with everything we will ever need in this life but still yearn for more.

I now have gained some goodness despite my stained soul. This often overwhelms me as an enveloping sense of well-being and graciousness fills me. This comes unexpectedly, suddenly, from somewhere suppressed deep within my being. And as rapidly as it appears, it then vanishes, leaving only the thought of goodness. With this, I know I can be good and do good. I also know I can live a just life if I choose to.

I have since used the power of the dormant goodness within me to break the bond that I have with my past. I, however, still cannot dispel the evil I have within. When I try, I become conflicted and lost. I find no peace or freedom, just pain, misery, betrayal, and death. As I try, this evil retaliates by devastating those I know. Everyone I once knew and all the love I once felt has long since withered and died, killed by this evil. I have lost everything by trying. It has since shattered me into submission. I simply cannot dispel this evil or break free from its grasp.

What is the point of continuing when everyone you knew and loved died? Life then becomes a continual struggle.

Karma has ensured I would need to be redeemed and forgiven to be freed. This, I will not know nor have the opportunity to live a peaceful or carefree life with love or comfort. My life will remain horrid and dark. All I can do is yearn to be saved and forgiven.

Often I see how others find love, peace, and happiness. All I can do is reminisce and shed sorrowful tears for all the things and feelings I would never know. Seeing this also reemerges old feelings with false hope that then prey on my mind. Haunting thoughts then add to my daily struggles, forcing me to harden my resolve and persevere with my miserable existence. And by knowing there will be no salvation for me and I will not be saved, I question the purpose of my life. I have to be realistic. I simply have to endure and persist while dispelling all the false hope that fills my mind with reprieve or leniency. I have to accept that love and hope will never rescue me or be part of my life. Nor will I find internal peace. I simply have to be satisfied with my own self-love.

A Forgettable Meeting

I find myself within a crowd of people, all frozen in place, standing, gazing into the distant horizon. As I slowly begin to move, those close to me turn, look at me and acknowledge me. These people possibly think I know them, and yet I don't recognise them.

Where am I? Have I lost my memory? Has someone placed me here?

I am certainly perplexed by what I see and hear. Several people approach and begin to talk to me, saying my name and asking personal questions.

Do these people know me? Is this a ruse?

As I look around, gazing at the people that surround me, I simply don't recognise anyone. As I keep looking, something stirs within, triggering some dormant thought and memory. As I look again, I begin to recognise some of these people. I realise I know these people. I have always known them. It took a while, but now I remember. The faces of these people are not from this time but a different era, from some past lived life.

Is this real? Is this the truth? How is this possible? Is this a gathering of old souls?

As I linger within this crowd, I attempt to converse by asking the people closest to me where I am. I see them poised to answer and then nothing. They freeze with a blank expressionless faces. I sense something has occurred that removed their thoughts. A sort of amnesia has enveloped them, taking their mind off elsewhere. It must be forbidden for sentenced souls like me to ask and know. I realise this, I cannot do; I cannot ask or discuss my journey with others. Only the chosen and redeemed can do so.

Is there something that makes us forget? Are we only able to recall dormant memories of our past with events, places, and people but not able to relay these to others? Are our memories linked to some alternate reality or some dream-state that appears with some type of mind control? Or are these imposed on us, implanted false memories? Is this how we are being manipulated and controlled? Is someone benefiting from this, by corrupting the truth with induced amnesia and implanted false memories? Or is this all part of a science experiment?

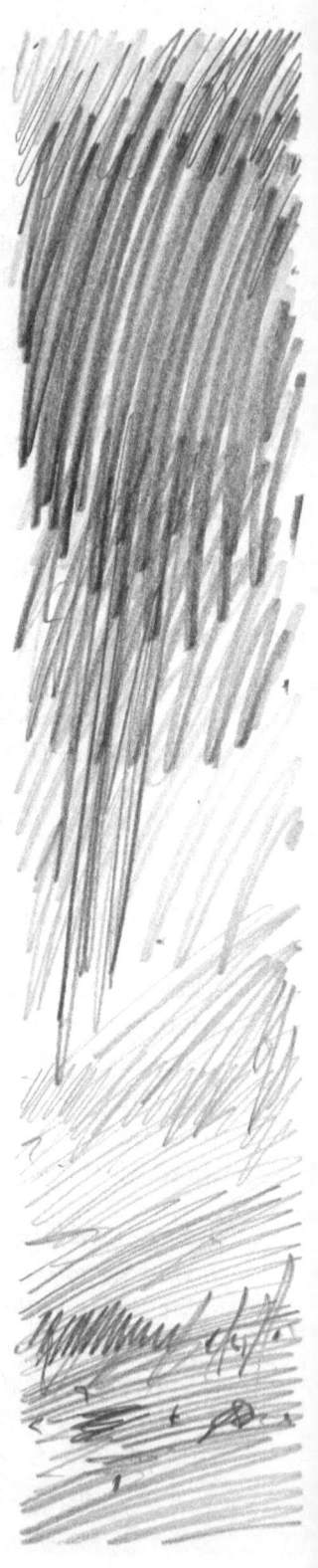

The Quest for Contentment
and Happiness

Prepare for the worst but hope for the best.

There are only horrid ancient memories that occupy my mind. All these give me grief as I am forced to remember so I don't forget what I had done. And I did wrong. I had participated in wrongdoings without questioning, without thinking, or considering the harm and hurt I would cause. And as I participated, I did not stop or help those in need. Nor did I see reason or try to halt the senseless trauma that occurred. I allowed others to manipulate me so I could do their evil bidding. This was the time I had allowed darkness and evil to enter my soul so as to dominate and control me. It then proceeded to unleash needless harm, violence, and destruction on earth. This then stained me.

I now know what happened and understand what I had done.

The stain I carry is a legacy left from all my past misdeeds. My deeds had accumulated substantial karmic debt, resulting in the stain, the evil I now have within me. This had forced karma to sentence me, so as to also stop and control the evil within me. But this evil persists and at times overwhelms, forcing me to again do its bidding. It is still powerful, albeit now desperately seeking to break free from karma which holds us both.

I know and feel this evil. I am its vessel. I have enabled it to unleash its misery and trauma on this plane. It cares for none, including me, having destroyed my family and life. My mother fled in fear when I was young. I saw the death of my two brothers and then felt the devastation this caused as it shattered my life.

I desperately tried to quell this evil but to no avail. I cannot stop what it does or what occurs. There is no respite for the horrors that it unleashes with the rampant havoc it causes. As this unfolds and happens, I am unable to stop, while karma monitors and holds me accountable for all that it does and occurs. I cannot change this; what occurs is not my doing. I simply have to learn to live with this, the evil, the stain within me.

Of the many choices granted to me in this life, none have helped me overcome this. Nor has my sentence or its many ordeals. Nor have I received help. This, I must do, I alone must dispel the evil I have inside.

Our Collective Social Debt

Sins can be forgiven with repentance when these are confessed and atoned.

The stain at La Mancha was pervasive. It affected many generations, all tempted with unholy desires that could not be resisted. The evil unleashed was comprehensive and relentless, completely overwhelming and devastating all in its path. As it spread, it consumed victims, stealthily, without revealing its presence or intentions. And despite this stain persisting for centuries on these lands, the only people that knew this, and felt it, were already damned.

The stain is a force that is felt and experienced. It comes as a heavy dark load burdening the soul as it enacts its curse, unleashing misfortune and misery. Some, like me, were stained at birth, while others became stained later in life by their misdeeds and sins.

Is this stain real? Does the stain affect us all similarly? Or is the stain a quirk of life, an illusion created by tales supported by false truths?

We all know God's plan, and we all know we must remain on the just path. But with free will, we can choose our life path and deviate from God's plan and disobey His will. But if we do, we then stain ourselves and begin accumulating karmic debt.

Each person sets their fate by their actions. And we, as a collective and race, set the global fate. What we do is what society does. And what society does is what we do. And if one falters and sins, then we all likely falter and sin together, as a society.

We are all in this together. This is why it is important to maintain on course and stay on the just path. We are all complicit, liable, and responsible for what occurs. And if we allow society to disregard and ignore God's law, thinking this will not affect us, we are then mistaken.

There is no excuse. We can't claim innocence by remaining ignorant, uninformed, and failing to stop what occurs. Rather, we become part of the problem. And if we allow our society to accumulate debt, then we also damn ourselves individually, collectively, and globally.

Consequential Outcomes

Can you see what is happening? Can you see how we all contribute to what is occurring? Can you not see the irreparable harm we are causing to the environment, to this planet, and thereby, also to ourselves? Can you imagine what could happen if this continues? And do you care if this causes total devastation?

As individuals, we are generally disinterested in what happens around us. Not seeing, not caring, we also fail to notice the global harm and consequences of our combined actions. Nor do we see the suffering of the disenfranchised. When we do look and see, our true nature reveals our arrogance with a self-centered, selfish disregard and refusal to accept any contributory liability or responsibility for what has occurred. And instead of helping, we think this is rightly deserved.

Without much regard or care, we are allowing the inevitable to occur. We are on a path that is taking this world to its tipping point, to a time when this planet will no longer be able to support us. But rather than acknowledging this, we conveniently choose to disregard and dismiss the science. We optimistically think we will be safe. We also think there will be alternatives, albeit imaginary, in false realities. We are simply fooling ourselves with rhetoric that disregards the truth and reality, the same as Don Quixote had done long ago.

Those who know what is at stake have accepted the awful truth. They have tried in vain to change the course we are on. They have desperately tried to also change our nature by fighting the stain directly. They know evil is leading us to the brink of destruction. They also know if we continue along this path, we all will be damned. These people are our true saviours. They care about our fate and have tried to place us on the just path. We should applaud their courage and selflessness but rather we choose to remain oblivious to this. We will only begin to understand when karma intervenes to take hold and make us accountable, as a collective, by sentencing us to purgatory.

Conversing with God

I seek and want forgiveness for everything!

The church decreed forgiveness for mortal sins can be obtained by confession, through the sacrament of penance, and by the purchase of a church-issued indulgence. With the sale of indulgence, the church had elevated itself to God's status, placing itself on equal footing as God.

Is it right for us to forgive one another? Isn't this God's work and prerogative?

The absolution of sin requires faith, conviction, and asking God for forgiveness. He is known to give unmerited, undeserved forgiveness by his grace. His mercy is infinite. There is no need or requirement to do or achieve anything else before we ask or receive forgiveness.

No matter how serious our sins are, God is always willing to forgive and give us a new and fresh start. However, we must do this as mortals. We must be prepared to redeem ourselves by atoning all our past sins. And despite seeking and receiving God's forgiveness, karma does not forget or forgive.

Forgiveness from karma must be earned by living life in penance, by redeeming ourselves. I had asked many times to be forgiven but was never truly forgiven. And by not redeeming myself and not atoning or reconciling past misdeeds, my sins were not forgiven. This had forced karma to sentence me. Karma brought me here, and by placing me at this time, it had also allowed me to reconcile what I had done. This is what I must do while I complete this sentence.

All I had done thus far and the life I have now lived has shown me that I will need several lifetimes to complete my sentence, be freed and forgiven. Time is all I have, which I must use wisely by repenting and atoning all the bad I had done, while I still can. This is my fate. This is what I must do now.

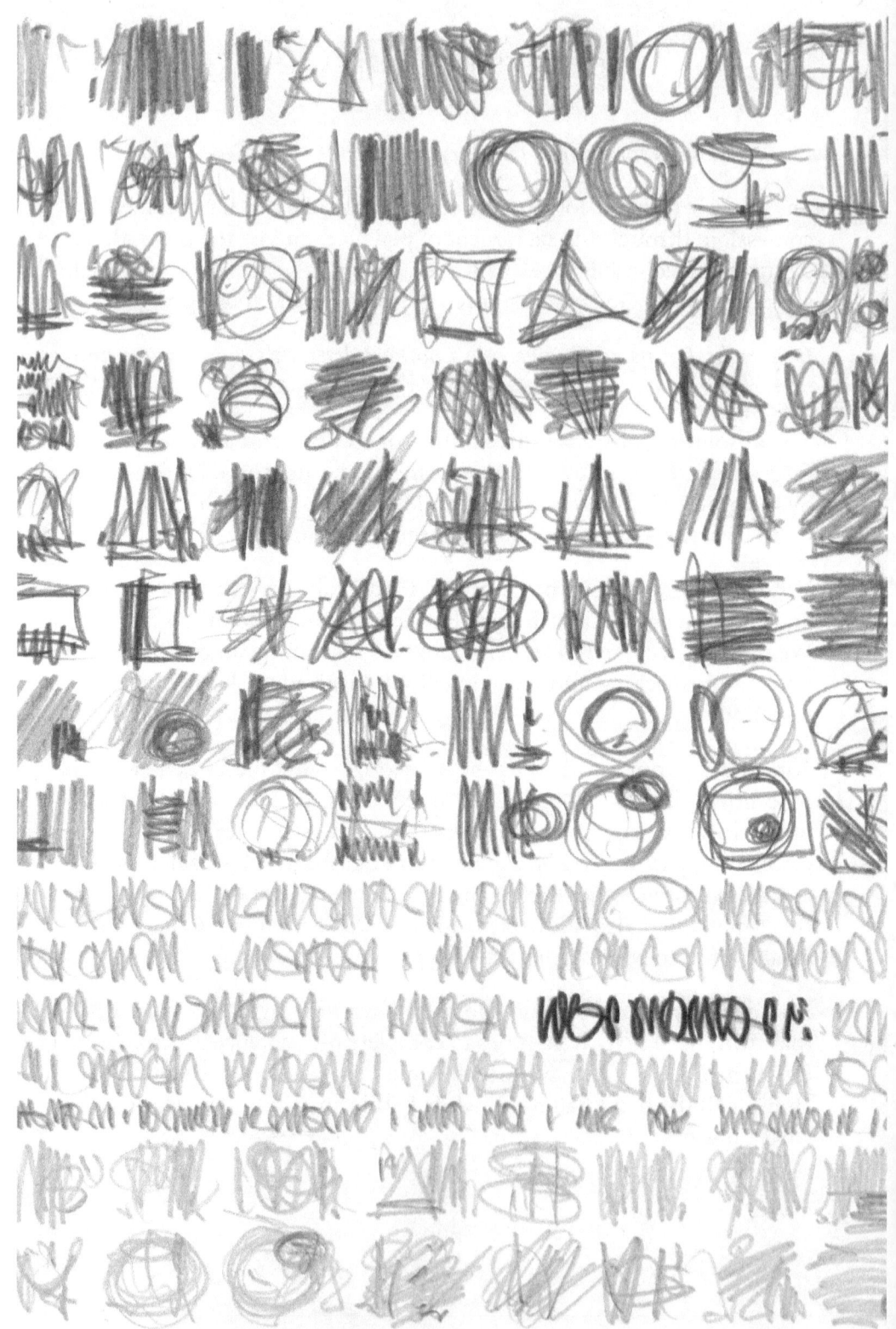

True Forgiveness

When will I find peace? Why does my suffering continue?

All that I ask Him remains unanswered. All I hear is deafening silence. This, however, speaks volumes to me.

I know I am not good nor perfect, nor have atoned for all my past sins. Nor am I living a just or good life. And yet I feel I deserve peace and forgiveness.

My past misdeeds were unconscionable. My sins were inexcusable and had justified my punishment. But living a life full of punishment is not what I had contemplated or can endure. I want this to change.

There was no dialogue, debate, or questioning with the judgement or sentence I received. When this was ordained, it could not be changed.

Is this just? Is a life full of suffering just punishment for things done in some past incarnation? Are you a vindictive God? How can I begin to understand you, Lord?

To begin to understand, I must first know my truth. This, however, has always eluded me. I will never know this. I am a mere mortal, and my understanding is limited. My mind does not have the capability or capacity to understand all there is. Nor can I begin to imagine or comprehend the vastness that exists. How can any mortal mind understand the finite with infinite, the mortal with immortal, and the temporal with eternal? To know this, I will need to transcend this life.

With this lingering thought, I satisfy myself by simply questioning the truth of my predicament. As I meditate, I concentrate and begin to focus on what is. Soon my mind clears, and I realise how unnecessary this is. This is just one fruitless interaction in this meaningless life that has no progression or purpose. I have placed myself here. All my self-imposed and accumulated negative impediments had stymied my progress and prevented me from seeing and realising my truth.

The Departed

I have always remembered the departed. Their memories occupy my every thought. I simply cannot forget, and nor can I dispel these thoughts. I have long known these people and will likely meet them again, possibly in the next incarnation. I always see their anguished faces, trying to be heard, understood, and freed. These are not merely thoughts as I also sense their presence. They are always close to me. Often I hear them. I remember their familiar voices, always reminding me of their horrors, which I cannot forget.

I must have harmed and traumatised these souls. I must have altered their lives, possibly with a premature death for some long-forgotten reason. Here, they exist as spirits, hovering in limbo, penetrating my mind at will. When they enter my thoughts, they fill me with their hatred and vengeance. They do this as they seek release from this eternal ordeal. I feel how determined they are as they push and prod me, forcing me to reconcile what I had done to them.

I simply abide by their wishes to appease them. I atone for what I can while desperately wishing they would stop haunting me. These are persistent souls that refuse to leave my mind.

Medication does not help. This only dulls my senses. It softens and dissipates some voices but not the memories or thoughts of dread and despair.

While I rest, these spirits take advantage of me. They take me to horrid and dark places so they can devour and consume me. I must, therefore, stay sober and vigilant, so I can prevent this. I must always use all my might and strength to remain in control. There is no respite for me. I cannot digress. Nor can I question to understand what they want. I simply must trust myself to remain on course and not falter or succumb to these voices. I must remain grounded, have courage, and use my strength to continue and endure. Only in death will I be able to dispel these tortured souls that occupy all my thoughts in my mind.

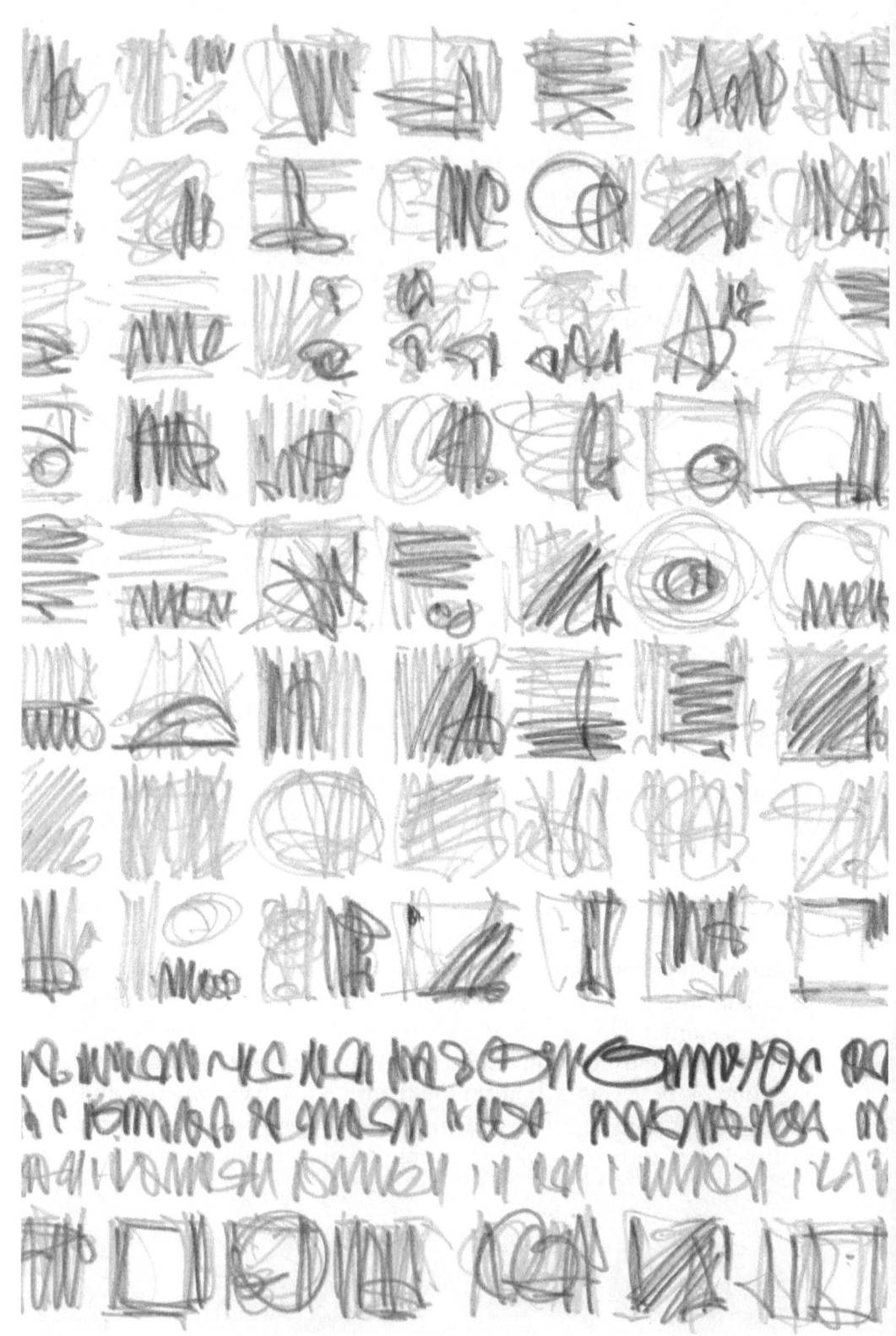

The Path to Enlightenment

All souls are immortal. Only the righteous are immortal and divine.

It is not living that is important but living rightly. True fulfilment and enlightenment can be achieved by living a just, true, and righteous life.

I now understand this. This is what I must do. I cannot continue to digress doing bad, as this has brought me here. I have no excuses and there are no excuses for what I have done and nor what I continue to do.

I know what is at stake, and there is a possibility I might fail. I must, therefore, continually remind myself to remain on the just path and do the right things while I complete my sentence. I must do this as I fear succumbing and damning myself for eternity. I have already suffered much, to reach here and cannot give up now.

This has been an arduous journey of change for me and I have changed. I no longer take life by its throat and force it to give me what I want. Nor do I now take without giving in return. With what has occurred and what I have endured, I still must complete this journey.

My existence and life are mere catalysts for the change I must undergo. The required change must be transformative for me to be saved. What I have done thus far, is still insufficient to be redeemed. I will need to muster inordinate amounts of energy and willpower to prevail. This I must do by being steadfast, focused, and resourceful. I must have the fortitude to endure this until its end. And when change does occur, I hope I will be able to endure what is to come and accept what occurs.

My life increasingly becomes harder as I undertake these challenges. I struggle to sustain what I have and must use all my might and strength to persevere, overcome, and reach the next goal. I simply cannot stop or rest. Standing idly or pathetically by would only worsen my dilemma and kill my resolve. I continue so, eventually, I will be able to reconcile all the bad I had done. As I persist, I use all I have learned to make appropriate choices and set things right. And when I do complete this journey, I will then know my perseverance had set free me.

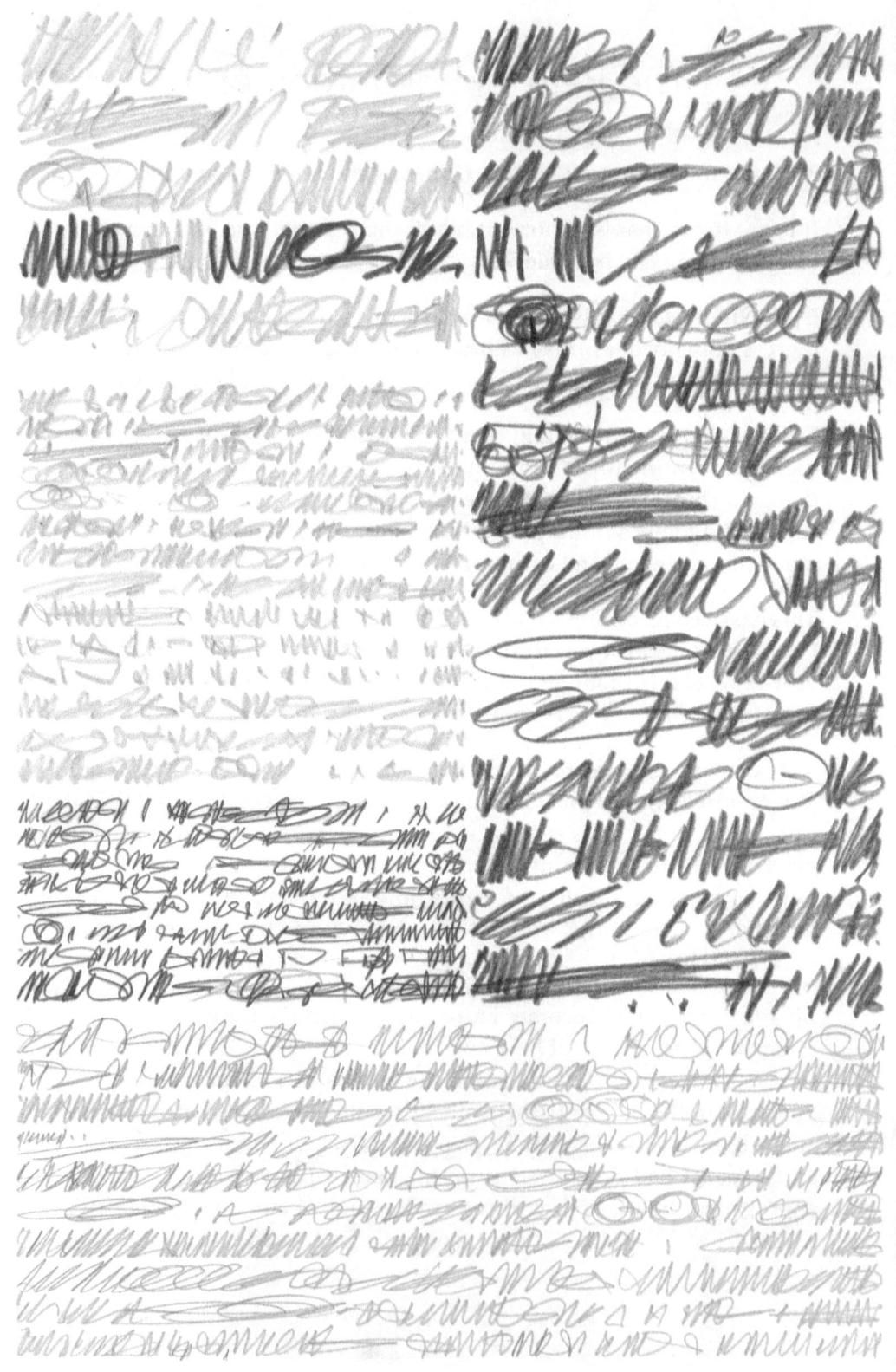

A Time to Set Things Straight

Life on this plane is bound by certain universal laws. These influence everything that occurs here, including everything we do. These set the path that leads life to its destiny. These determine who we are, become, what we do, and how we are to live life. We, however, do have choices. We can choose not to abide by these laws to cause chaos and imbalances, and unleash evil on earth. It may then however, take generations, but eventually, these laws will catch up with us and force us to reconcile what we had done. I had done this, and now I am paying the price. I must now abide by these laws while I seek redemption. To stay on the path, I must not succumb to temptation or desire and not corrupt my thoughts with false hope. I must tread carefully and thoughtfully to progress. I know every step and everything I do matters. I, however, must remain positive in mind and spirit and with everything I do. Only by remaining true and abiding by these laws, I will improve my circumstances and progress to reach freedom. This I do by following ten guiding principles:

1. Reconcile all the harm and trauma I had caused others.

2. Reconcile my traumas, including the pain I felt and endured during childhood.

3. Reconcile failed relationships and end dysfunctional associations.

4. Reconcile my finances; settle accounts and forgive debts.

5. Remember what needed to be remembered and record this for posterity.

6. Say the things that needed to be said.

7. Do some good with every action and deed.

8. Free myself from all material burdens and hindrances.

9. Free myself from temptation and the desire to sin.

10. Lose everything including my life, so I can be reborn again, free.

As I progress, new thoughts seed in my mind. Soon I see a new reality unfold before me, revealing a different truth. The change that then occurs instantly dispels my fears and selfishness. I feel goodness grow within, improving my well-being and those around me. I now know I am on the right path.

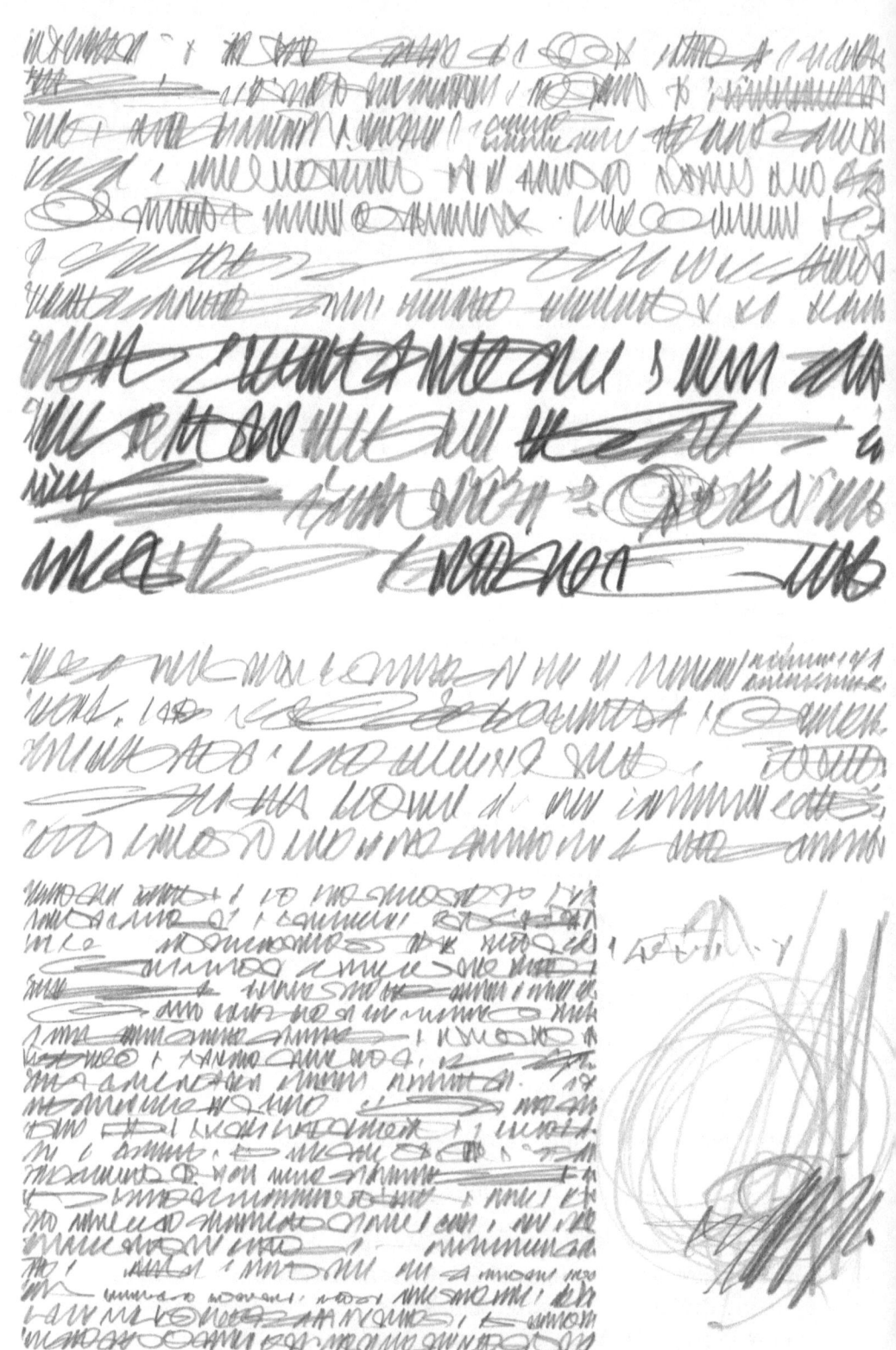

Seeing and Realising the Self

I had long lost my way. I had ventured too far into an unknown. I had entered the forbidding territory. Here, all I feel and see is endless grief.

A huge chasm has opened in front of me, widening, threatening to consume me. I must traverse this to reach the other side. Everything I do does not help but rather widens this chasm, making it unbridgeable. I have since lost the opportunity to reconcile this. I have lost my way. This mind maze has trapped me.

I am ordinary like everyone else. I have the same genetic makeup but don't feel the same or equal. I know I am different. I am tainted and stained with evil inside.

There is no recourse or discussion or medicine to be taken, nor is there a facility where I can be placed on a recovery path. I must simply endure my condition and dilemma. I can only react to circumstances as these occur. I cannot plan or set goals. My mind keeps failing me, I cannot think clearly or make appropriate decisions. I cannot comprehend or understand why this has happened or what is happening. All my connections with the present have severed along with everything and everyone I knew. I am truly lost and cannot recover. With my life devoid of meaning and substance, I can only wait for some change to occur and remedy this.

I am not a righteous or just person. I have always lived with sin. Greed with lustful desires for material things was always in my mind. This has driven me to attain wealth and power but left me isolated and abandoned in this predicament. This is my own doing, my choice. My selfish stubbornness brought karma into my life to sentence me. I had willed this on me, purposefully, so I would change and transcend this state of my being. There was no other choice. I would not otherwise atone or repent the harm I had caused. Nor could I progress.

Now sentenced, I question and validate everything to avoid again succumbing to some dark evil tenancy that will damn me further. I need to find and align myself with the sacred virtues and rites of the divine. I need also to gain wisdom and understanding to find ways to dispel the evil I have inside so I can finally redeem myself. Knowing this, I have gained a glimpse at the full and ugly truth of my condition.

Caged Choice

Time has inextricably tied the past and present with the future. All have become part of a continuum of things. There is uncertainty and unpredictability with our future as things cannot be foretold, and yet we can also be fated.

Our destiny is set before birth and determines who we are, who we become, what we do, along with all our thoughts, ambitions, and what we are to achieve. This cannot be changed. What was, is, and will be are set as part of the divine plan. And whether we don't achieve or do what was fated in one lifetime, this simply is carried to the next. This is part of the divine plan, our fate, and our destiny, along with all that was, is, and will be.

As much as our lives are foretold, so is who we become, all our beliefs, actions, and achievements. All these follow the set universal laws of cause and effect, compensation, gestation, and the perpetual transmutation of energy. With these laws, what is and will be, have ensured balance and equilibrium will be maintained on this physical plane.

The free will and choice gifted to us is a mere illusion. It is simply impossible to change what has been preordained. Our life's course and fate follow set motions that place us en route to be where we always were meant to be. Each life lived has this preset destination. Deviations to the plan are rare, occurring only with temporal disruptions that soon have some cosmic intervention. We, thereby, are always drawn back to fulfil our destiny.

I deviated from the divine plan by allowing evil to rule me and change my destiny. Evil manipulated time and space and took me out of the divine plan. This freed me, allowing me to venture unhindered well beyond my destined set path. It then took an eternity for karma to find me and restore the imbalance I had caused. Karma then reached back, tallied all my past misdeeds, judged me, and sentenced me. This is why I am fated to live this miserable life and forced to reconcile all the bad I had done while I live with this judgement.

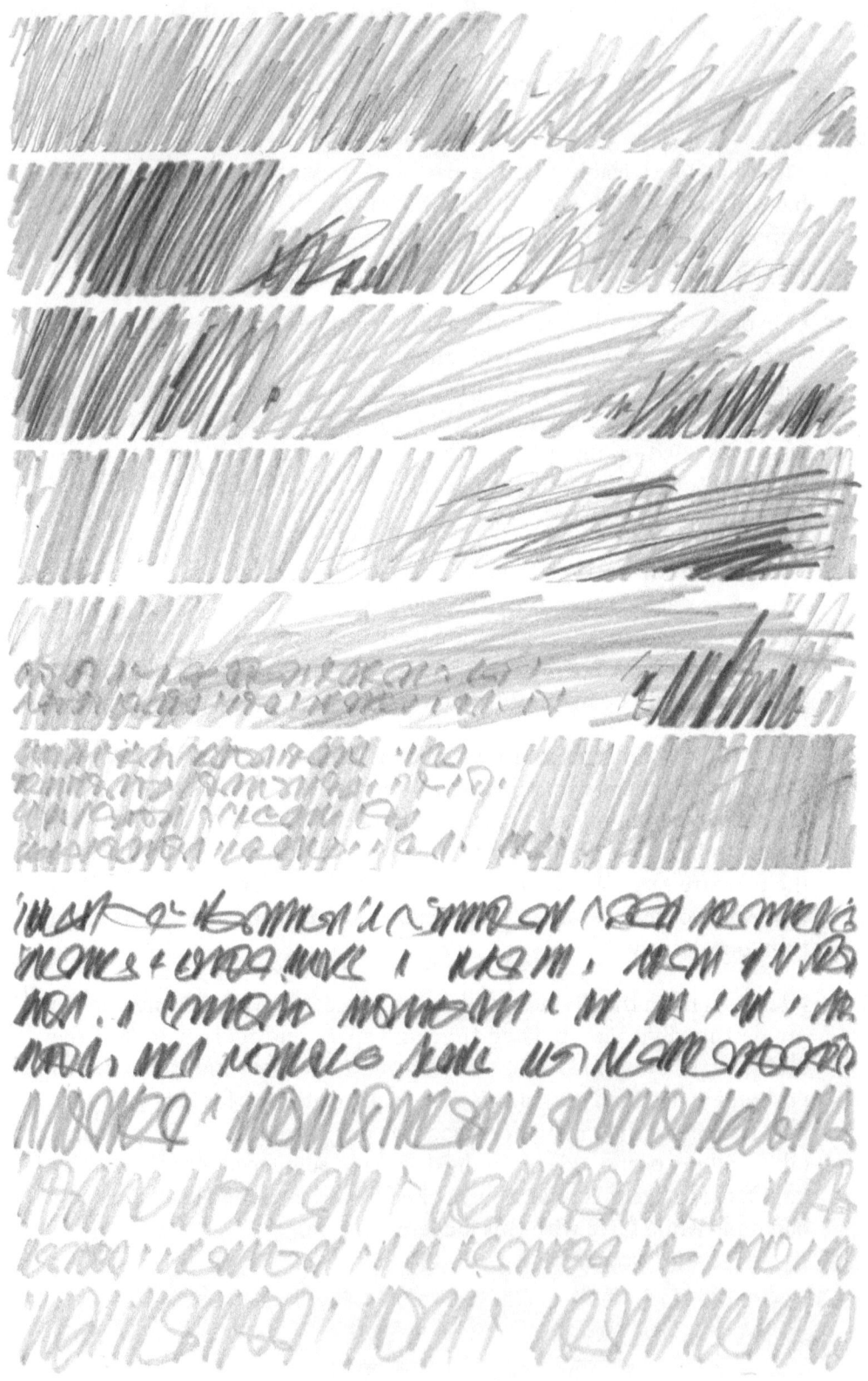

Love and Forgiveness

When I still longed for love and company, my heart broke. As I recovered, my heart mended twisted, and it hardened. This changed me. I then sought to find someone with a heart as damaged and broken as mine.

Love is strange. Great joy and comfort can be accompanied by an equal amount of pain, misery, and grief.

The vacuum that love leaves when it wanes and dies can easily be replaced with hurt, resentment, and hate. Life then can become unbearable. Relationship tension can escalate, changing circumstances, so togetherness becomes irreconcilable. The only remaining thing to do is leave this behind; the harmful and toxic environment.

Separation avoids further escalation, retribution, and bad behaviour. Separation takes us to the other end of love – to a lonesome and isolated place without happiness or companionship. There, we are forced to confront ourselves so we accept who we are. There, we must battle with our demons until we reach contentment with what we still have. There, we must find self-respect, self-love, self-worth, and dignity to keep us whole and sane. With these, we can continue with the drudge of life and gain some purpose. And with these, we can slowly purge all our lingering ill feelings, the raw and sad emotions, before these worsen and harm us. And if we happen to lose this battle, then undoubtedly, feelings of abandonment, disappointment, and disillusionment will then overwhelm us. Undoubtedly, it is better to have loved than not. Also, it is better to have known someone than not. Knowing this, we then need the courage to forgive, acknowledge, and accept what was and what is meant to be. This acceptance gives us the absolute truth that guides us, allowing us to unshackle ourselves from our past and leave behind the burden we had carried while resurrecting hope to continue to our destiny. Then, at our lives' end, we undoubtedly will desperately yearn for forgiveness. We will become needy, seeking caring, compassionate friendships, people who will respect us and not judge us.

We then want to forget our past and be absolved from our sin. We don't want to deal or negotiate as we seek unreserved forgiveness. Only this can mend our broken heart, as this also assures us that we still have some goodness inside, despite all the bad we had done.

Paralysed

I had reincarnated here to pay my karmic debt. I am, therefore, captive, sentenced; this is my life and fate. I am unable to change this, nor can I end this. All I can do is persevere and ponder this, my dilemma. As this thought lingers in my mind, I become transfixed, thinking about what was, is, and could be.

At age 50, I again felt invincible, courageous, and righteous for having persevered through the toil of a selfless and repentant adult life. Only once before, previously, when I was young, I sensed and acted on such a rebellious thought. Thinking back to that time gave me the courage and filled me with self-entitlement. Thinking I deserved more and wanting an early reprieve, false hope encouraged me to act.

Everything then changed. I rebelled and broke free. I dismissed karma and let evil take me. Karma, however, soon intervened, retaliated, and I felt its wrath. I found myself hit by a fast-moving vehicle, leaving me paralysed. Now bedridden, as I think back, I realise this was a mistake.

This accident incapacitated me, worsening my dilemma. I now live in a lifeless body and need people to look after me and care for me, to ensure my body keeps functioning. I lay here with many similar-fated people, all suffering equally. This place is devoid of pity. Everyone here is overwhelmed with their worries which occupy all their thoughts. The trauma felt here never ceases or ends, this, we must all endure.

I wish I could end this but cannot. My horrid past has since paled into insignificance. I now realise how lucky I was. I had freedom, albeit sentence freedom. Now, I no longer can move or do what I want.

All the horrid thoughts that used to occupy my mind have strangely disappeared. And all the damned souls that occupied my mind seem to have manifested into this reality. They are here, with me, as my carers, free to unleash their vengeance on me. They have waited an eternity to find me in this vulnerable condition which they use now to punish and torment me. As I lay here, unable to move, I suffer greatly from what is done to me. This is my new reality, I cannot escape. This, I must endure.

Life as an Invalid

Here, I feel the vibrancy of life, and yet there is a stench of death.

There exists overwhelming hopelessness here. I am traumatised by this place. I also fear the people here, who purposefully unleash their vengeance on me. My mind has been consumed with fatalistic negativism. It has gripped and engulfed me, dominating my every thought. This, I wish to dispel and find that eternal slumber of inactive forgetfulness.

Sickness and ill health have followed me here. Paralysed, I simply lay motionless, trying to recall what was, when I was stronger, carefree, and active. I know there is no hope or cure for me, and I seek no help.

Bedridden, I allow my condition to progressively worsen as I feel my body deteriorate into nothingness. Carers hover around me, doing what they want. I am their unwilling captive as they unleash their retributive anger on me. There is no mercy. My life has become this.

I wallow in self-pity, waiting for my mind to clear, so again to fill me with some false hope. There, I find myself freed. There, I also find relief with new glimmers of hope. I then take my thoughts to where I want to go, entering an altered, different reality. There, I see a better, brighter future, which strengthens me and allows me to sufficiently recover so I can continue to endure my predicament. There, I have also seen how one day soon, I will again rejoin society as a valued member. Deep within, however, I know this will never eventuate. I will not recover, and nor will I leave this horrid and miserable place alive.

Is this how my life will end? Will anger, aggression, suffering, and pain continue to my end?

As I feel my mind free itself from my body, all my worldly and selfish desires vanish. Freed, I begin transcending my condition and find myself in spirit. Here, I find hope and begin to understand what is sacred and true. I know this place. I have been here before. This is the place where I will find redemption.

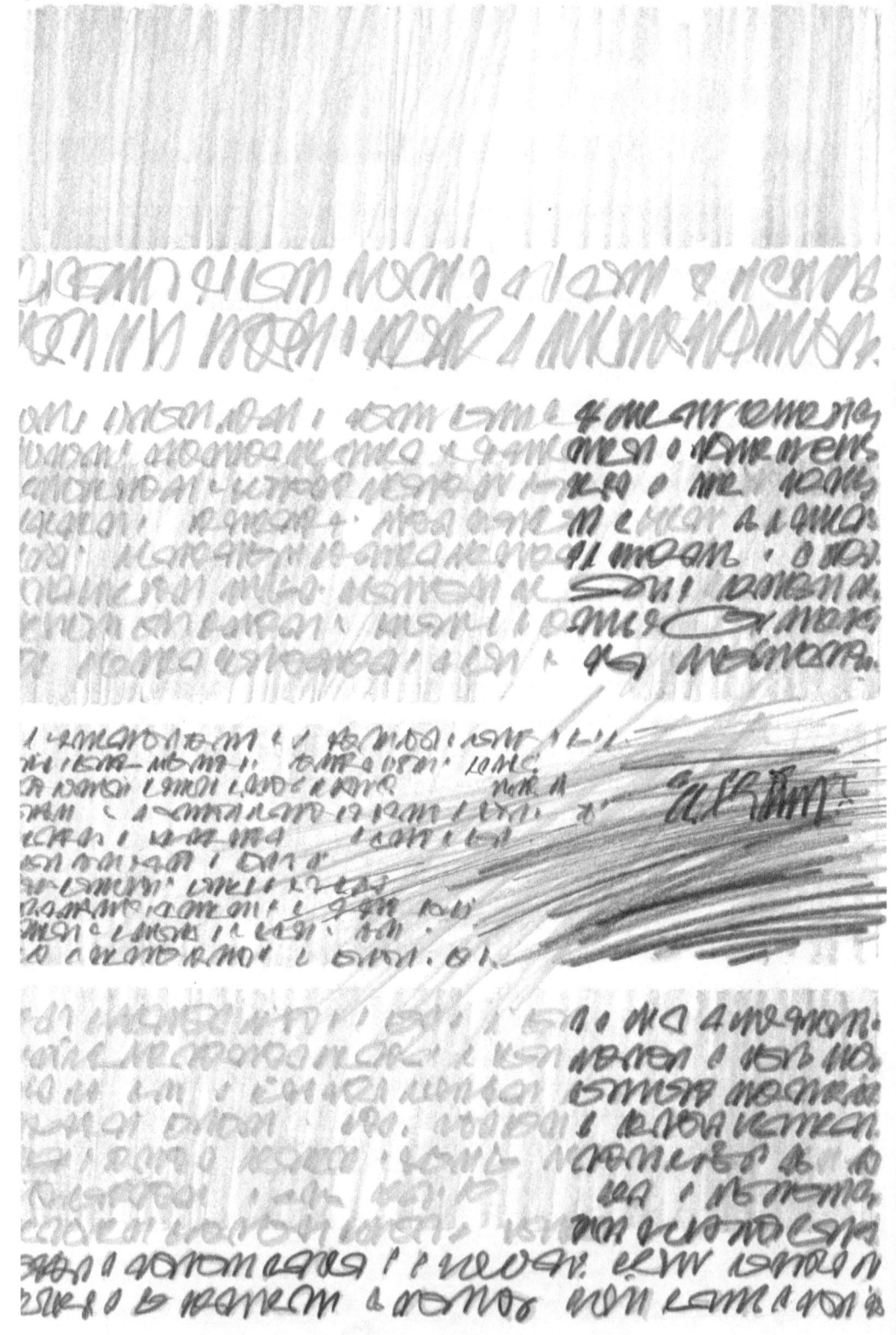

Gaining Freedom

In this retirement home of life, I live within a churn machine. This place leads the living to their ultimate destination. It takes the aged and infirmed on a set path, a self-driven conveyor journey that ends at its precipice. There is no return, reprieve, or leave from this. Everyone must make this final journey.

I see bewildered people outside, some looking in, some seeing this place in wonderment, while others wish they too could join us here. No one seems to understand or know what this place is or does. Some think it is an elitist aged club, while others see this as a destination for them to visit. As people arrive, the newcomers eagerly seek to integrate and assimilate into this residential culture of inaction. As they join, I notice them frantically trying to stay current, on the side of the living. Their time has become precious as they realise they have just arrived at their journey's end.

No, this is not an ideal way to end life, but it is where I have been placed. This place has since become my haven and it is here, I will meet my end. I no longer hope or think about how to improve my life as I have already resigned myself to the inevitable. I just lay here, staring up at the white ceiling, waiting for my end to come.

I endure this without privacy. Many people pass me by. Some I remember, but most are newcomers, people I had not yet met or seen before, knowing also, for every new face, an older has departed. I, however, no longer bother to acknowledge or remember faces anymore. I only wonder whether the departed found what they were looking for and whether their journeys' end was everything they wished and expected.

Realising the Truth

I feel that I am not worthy. My outward appearance expresses and reflects my condition and predicament. My incapacitated body tempts others to disrespect me and take advantage of me. This they do without respect or pity for me. As I am prodded, my pain surges through my body, filling me with misery and despair.

When I first arrived, I felt this place met my needs. I saw caring people and felt respected. When I decided to stay and settled, things quickly changed. Then the awful plain truth revealed itself as my life became arduous and difficult.

I thought I was capable, strong-willed, and determined. I also thought people here would help me find solace, peace, and meaning. And I thought I would be able to contemplate life and be content. This was what I thought and sought while forgetting I still had to repay a karmic debt.

I should have realised long ago that my reality and condition would never change. All I hoped and wished for would never eventuate as this was not ordained. I would never find peace or contentment in this life. The only comfort I have ever known and will ever know is in my head, residing in my thoughts.

This life, my existence, has been reduced to my sanity and worth. This is all I am and have. This is also everything this life has given me, which I will take to my end.

This life has since exhausted me. It has almost extinguished my essence. I no longer lust for life. I no longer have that unquenchable desire for more. I am resigned. I simply let this burdened horrid life take me to its end. And while I wait, all I do is exist.

Repentance and Atonement

I had made all the reparation that I could for all the wrongdoings I had done. I truly regret all the harm, injury, and death I had caused. I had atoned and reconciled all I could. I had done this while knowing this would never be enough. Atonement, redemption, and forgiveness were always beyond my reach. I must, however, continue, repent and make amends for as long as I can.

I had truly damned myself. There is no hope for me. I had diverged from the just path and burned bridges. I had ensured there was no way back. If I could, I would change this.

I know, I am not alone, and this is not a unique tale. Many people are living similar-fated lives. We are the unforgiven. We know we will never be reprieved. We are all sentenced, with a karmic debt to pay. We are also all punished, forced to live a miserable existence, so we suffer greatly for all the harm we had caused. We are also forced to persevere, unable to shorten our penance, as we are taught life's many lessons. I hope others will also write their asemic tales so someday, when combined, this world will know how damned we all are.

As I contemplated this, I begin to realise that the purpose of my life was to be punished. There was never any hope for me. I was never to receive what I sought. I would never find freedom or be forgiven. This would always elude me. To be forgiven, I will need to live an eternity of lifetimes, each being virtuous, righteous, always atoning for having enticed evil within me.

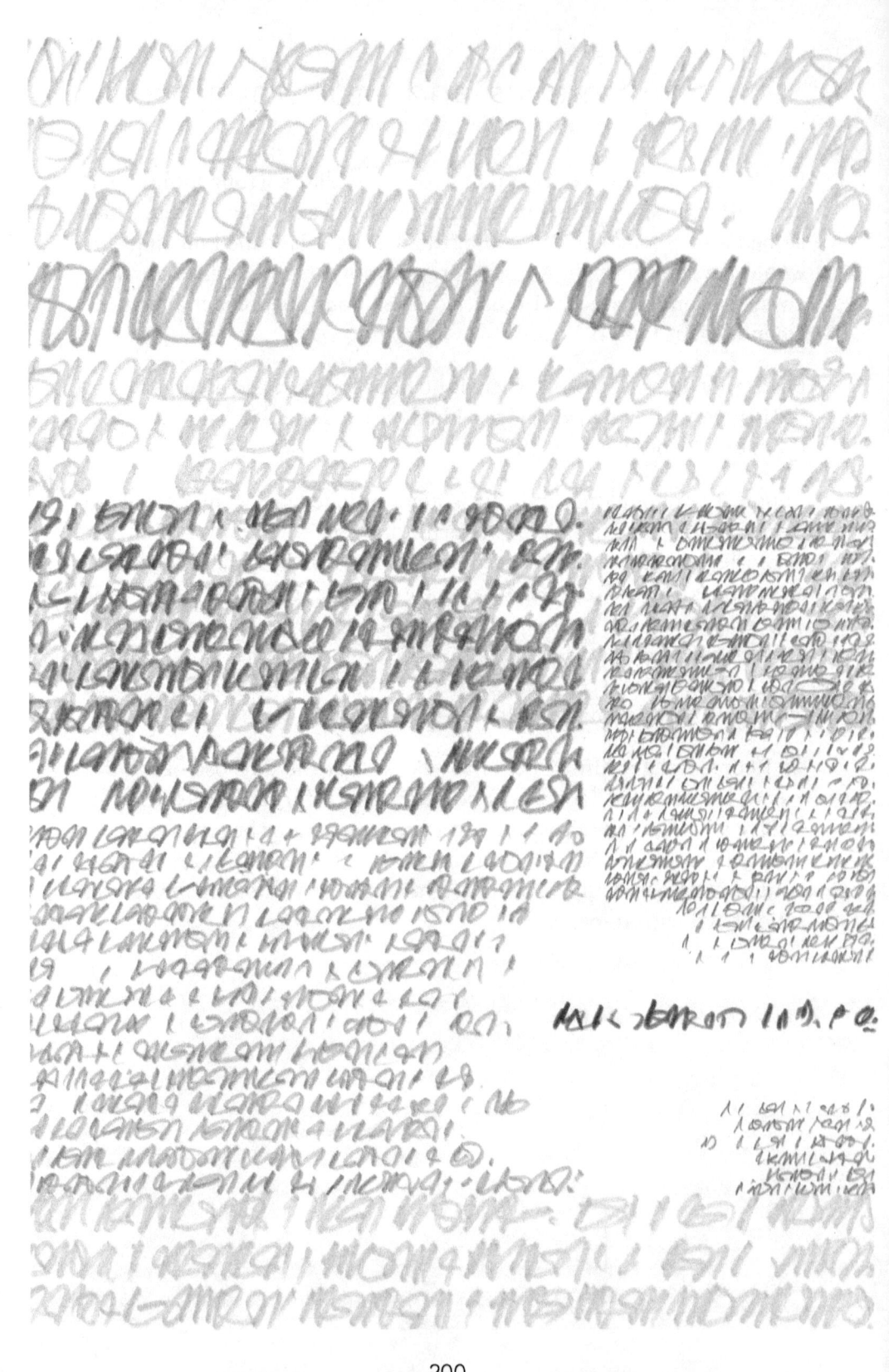

200

Absolution

Sure, I was bad and evil, but not in this lifetime.

Unable to move, I lay here in this semi-comatose condition. My life is intolerable. I have exhausted my second sight. I can no longer see what was, and nor do I care or seek further understanding with this life.

I did all I could with the time I had. I was fortunate. This lifetime allowed me to repent and atone for my past sins. This, however, was an insurmountable feat that I could not complete.

Each day I lived seemed an eternity. This had become an unending game of patience that I was forced to endure while I persevered, performing meaningless tasks. I had to remain calm as I was determined to reach here. Now I have inactivity to endure while I wait for my sentenced life to reach its end.

With the time I had, I was able to understand how my past, with all its misdeeds, ill thoughts, and evil intentions, had stained me and forced karma to intervene. All my past misdeeds had outlived my flesh and body. And these continued to accumulate through the countless incarnations I had lived.

I now understand how close life is tied to the order of things. I have seen how life is ruled by the law of opposites, duality, and correspondence, all placed here to ensure good and evil, death and life, and past and present are balanced. Karma is the enabler, intervening as required to ensure life remains aligned with the divine plan. This is why I am sentenced, to stop the enduring evil that I have carried within me for an eternity. Only death will absolve this incarnation of me from this.

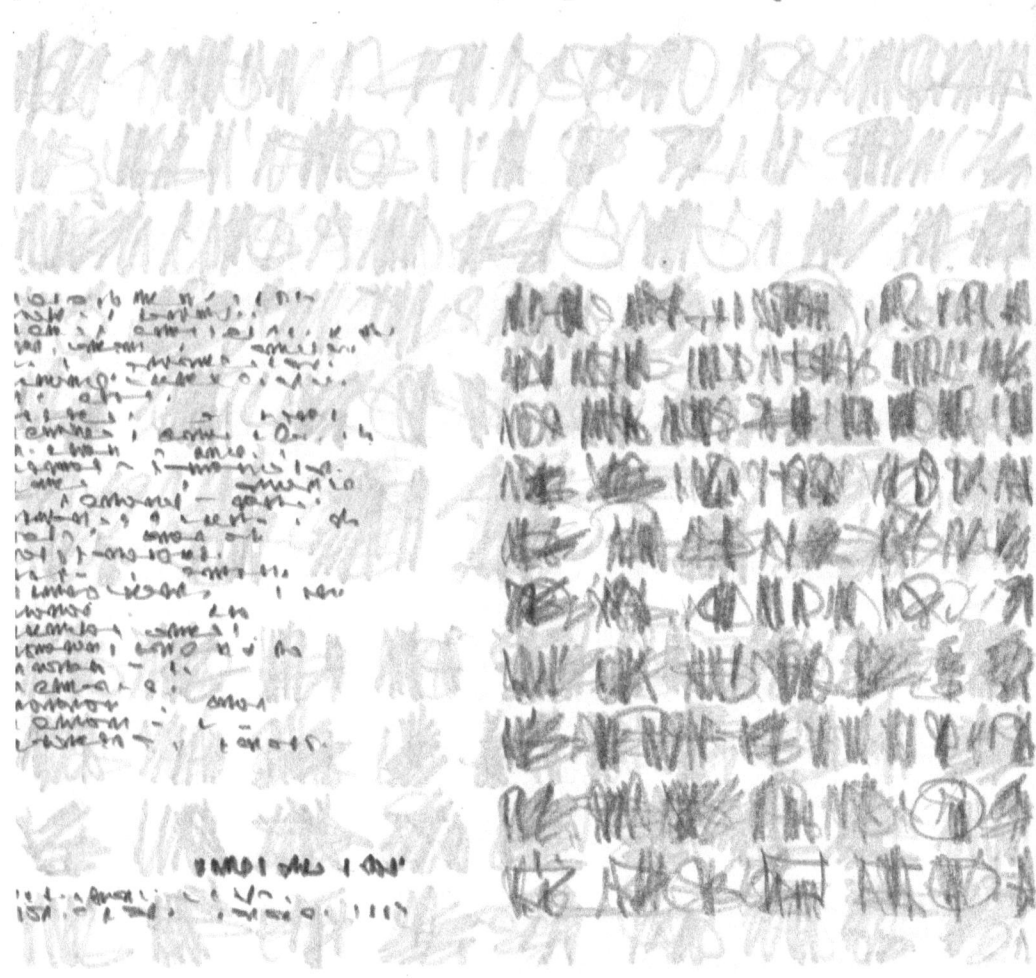

The End

When I leave, don't say a word; just accept this is the way things are and will be. In time, just reflect, and be contented with the friendship we had.

As I lay here, I feel weak; my life is ending. I sense the divine oneness is close. I have no fear. I am content. I no longer feel trapped or miserable. I feel truly connected with everything there is. I have now paid my karmic debt. Soon I will find peace.

As I lay here, I feel like some relic of a distant miserable past. Who I am, reveals itself with my scarred and aged body. What people see is a withered soul, waiting patiently for death to come. No one helps or tries to make me comfortable. There is no interaction. Nor do I want to shorten my miserable life. This unconscionable act would add to my karmic debt that someday I would need to also reconcile. I never again want to corrupt or stain my soul or damn myself.

As each day passes, I continue to pray, confess, and repent my past sins. I have not yet received forgiveness. I know I don't deserve any. All I can hope for is to accumulate some goodwill with the time that remains as this would greatly help me in my next life. Karma may then grant me some reprieve so I can set and achieve life goals, possibly live freely and choose how and where I live, be it righteous or not. This is, however, wishful thinking. As I contemplate this, memories of my past misdeeds resurface. I have no fear. It is also too late to regret. My end is near.

Patience got me here. I needed to live this life so I could discharge my karmic debt. This is how balance is kept, maintained, and how life thrives on this plane. Karma punished me as a wrongdoer. It forced me to reconcile and atone for the bad I had done. This is how I am to be redeemed. This is how life progresses along this continuum of things.

Along this path, eventually, I know I will find redemption with true freedom. Then I will also know I will be close to leaving this repetitive cycle of life, ending this damned human experience.

Premonition

Our ancestors set our present path. They had taught us to be self-centered, inward-looking, and mean-spirited. They had established this life for us. We are their reflection, and unquestioning, we follow in their footsteps. What they thought and aspired to, we now think and aspire to. We live with what they created and established long ago. This has become us; it is our life.

We do have choices and opportunities. We can decide whether we continue with their legacy or not. Change, however, is difficult. We cannot simply erase our past to start again. Change requires patience and determination to achieve. We must use our intellect collectively to reset the life we all live. And if we were to do this, we must bring everyone with us, including the most vulnerable and disenfranchised.

With the change we choose, we must stop harming the nonhuman world. We must learn to curb our indulgences and greed so we protect life and the environment. We must rein in our wants so we can transcend our self-centeredness and finally, separate ourselves from the evil that exists. We can choose to change the way society is structured by applying our intellect and technologies so these connect us all with what is real and important. By doing so, we may just be able to repair the global harm our forebears caused.

We are not bystanders. We are connected to all that exists and are complicit with all that occurs. We also have a responsibility to do good and not cause harm. We should know without real change, we will soon pass the threshold that then tips us all into some abyss. Compounding this is the karmic debt we also incur as individuals and as a society. And because of the global scale and the enormity of what we are doing, what is likely to occur will end with worldwide misery, misfortune, and calamity. This will then becomes our collective reality which will take generations to recover, possibly the same time it took to cleanse La Mancha, some 700 years.

That Night

Who is not a tortured soul?

That night the story of Don Quixote reminded me that there was no escape from reality. I then sensed this was the time and this night, my journey would end.

I soon drifted off to sleep, only to awaken suddenly, feeling my heartbeat slow and my breathing become fainter and shallower. I open my eyes but found my sight fading. Nothingness soon became me. Strangely, I felt at peace as my mind cleared and thoughts emptied.

As I stirred, I knew the end was near. Tiredness soon overwhelmed me, and I began to dream. I was back at my childhood home. I looked up and saw a small gap in a blinded window. A sliver of sunshine began to emerge, travelling across the room, stopping at my feet. Then the fog that had surrounded me began to dissipate and reveal a new truth and reality.

Jolted, I awoke. Was this a dream?

I looked at the wall and saw a clock as the minute hand struck the hour. New memories then flooded my mind as I regained my senses. I began to remember. I was not La Mancha. That was not my reality nor my life. I led a simple common life. I was not hindered, sentenced, or controlled by karma. I was an ordinary, calm, and law abiding individual.

Today I had work to do. I had appointments, people to meet, and things to do. This was my reality and my life.

Pausing to reflect, I contemplated and felt I had seen the truth. I also sensed that I had felt the presence of divine oneness. I then knew I was part of the divine plan. With this, I felt blessed.

I then thanked Don Quixote and prayed for his soul. I sensed his spirit had entered my mind to reveal universal truths. This also showed me what I must do. I must change so I can lead a just existence. To do so, I must reconcile my past, transcend my weaknesses and seek forgiveness for my past sins.

Epilogue

These asemic writings tell the tale of La Mancha, a stained soul living a life of penance. This tale has its origins deep in ancient history, predating the story of Don Quixote de La Mancha. It is a centuries-old tale that has seeded itself within asemic writings, having since germinated in word and print to reveal this story to the world. Within this tale is a past filled with trauma, grief, and horror that have festered for eternity, only to surface with the person called La Mancha.

La Mancha is travelling along the path called life, tempted by evil and sentenced by karma, forced to repent and atone for past sins. La Mancha has a corrupted soul that carries the fear of eternal damnation. This journey is of endurance and perseverance, requiring vigilance and care not to stain or allow evil to divert us with sin. This is a story that takes life to its very end.

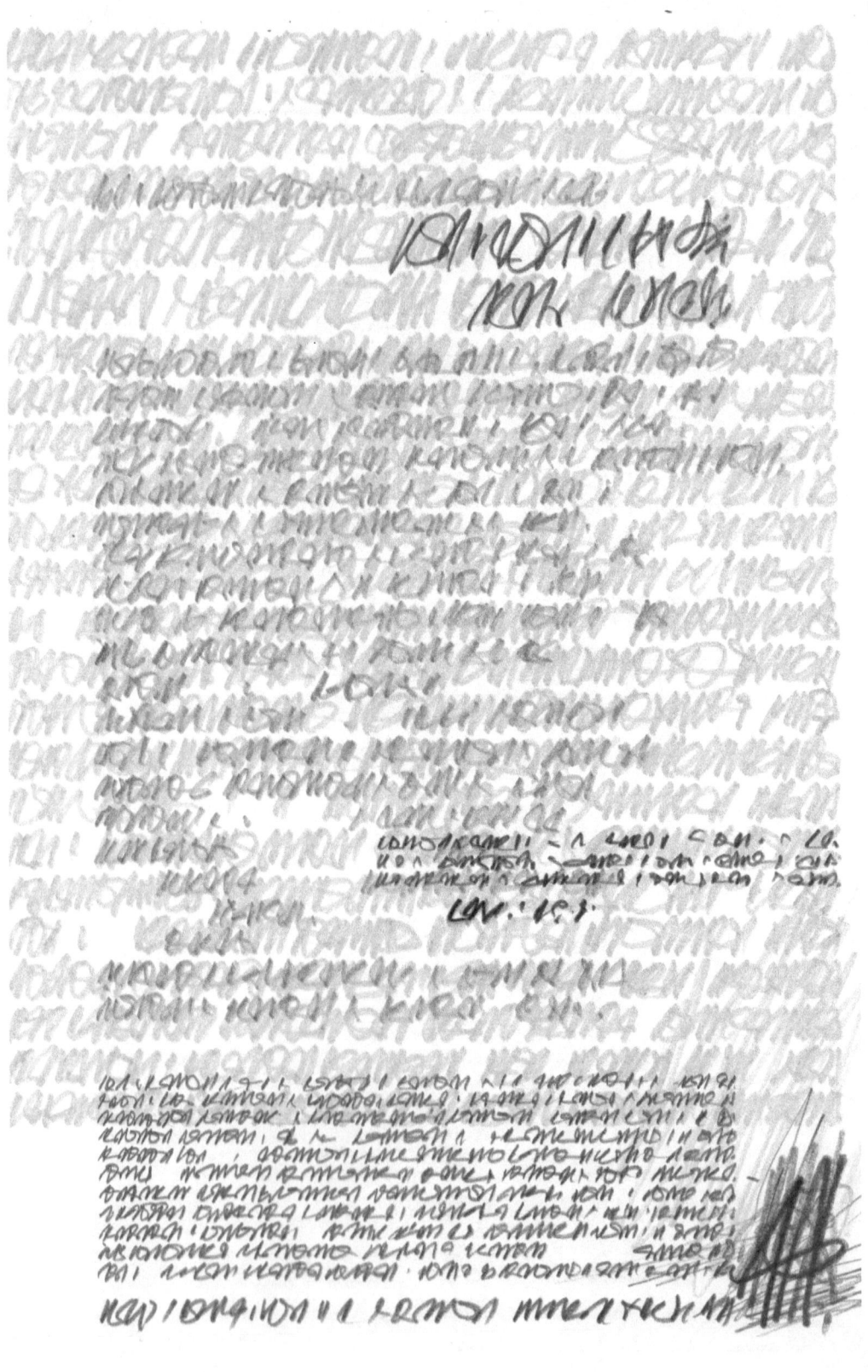

The Book And Tale

Is this the truth or a fable?

There are many coded messages within these asemic writings. Each page, image, and text tell its own age-old story, the tale of La Mancha.

This tale reveals our stained past and how we all are inextricably linked and connected to history, religion, politics, and wars. Our history is tainted with temptation, always succumbing to desires that entice and then overwhelm. As we falter, we sin and do evil. We then need to find redemption to be forgiven and to be able to progress further along the divine path.

Entwined in this tale is La Mancha's past, the many incarnations and lives lived sinning with misdeeds. Each past sin and misdeeds had stained La Mancha's soul so to be sentenced and forced to atone, reconcile, and pay an accrued karmic debt.

Can we be so tied to our past? Can we be held accountable for the bad we had done during past reincarnation? Does karma oversee all we do? Does karma exist? Are there consequences to doing bad? Can we freely live with sin? Why do we continue to cause harm to each other and the environment? Why are we not helping those fleeing persecution and wars?

These questions answer themselves as we read the La Mancha tale. The revealed reality is a frighteningly-familiar tale. We have all heard whispers of this tale, and it is one we all can relate to. It sheds light on the starkness of life while revealing plain truths.

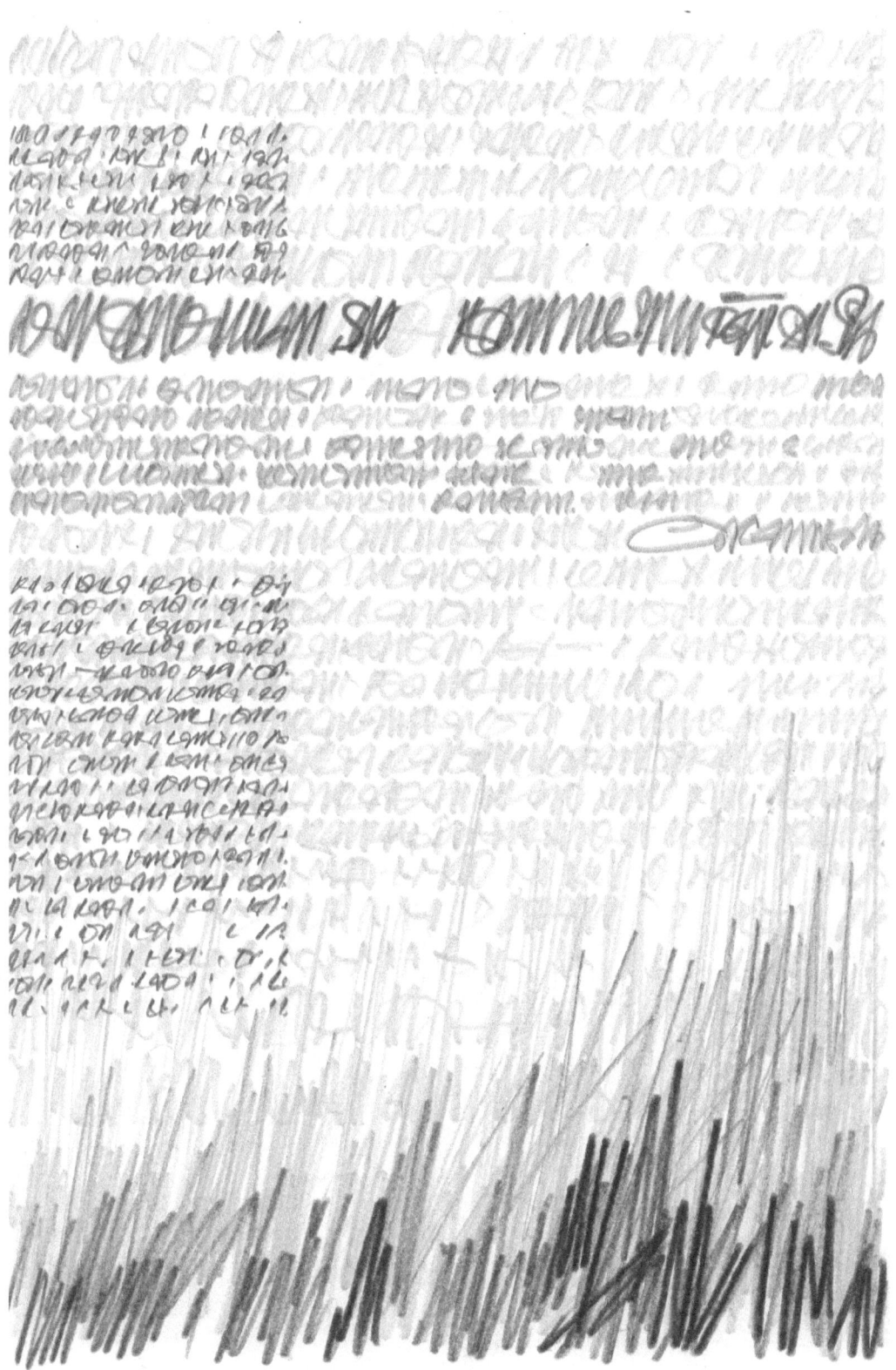

Index